COVID-19, Gangs, and Conflict

Front Cover Image: Image of SARS-CoV-2 the novel coronavirus that causes COVID-19. Source: Centers for Disease Control and Prevention (CDC). 2020, https://phil.cdc.gov/Details.aspx? pid=23311. [Public Domain].

COVID-19, Gangs, and Conflict

John P. Sullivan and
Robert J. Bunker, Editors

A Small Wars Journal—El Centro Reader

Copyright © 2020 by Small Wars Foundation. 805425

All rights reserved. No part of this book may be reproduced or transmitted in any form or by any means, electronic or mechanical, including photocopying, recording, or by any information storage and retrieval system, without permission in writing from the copyright owner.

The views expressed in this work are solely those of the author and do not necessarily reflect the views of the publisher, and the publisher hereby disclaims any responsibility for them.

To order additional copies of this book, contact:
Xlibris
844-714-8691
www.Xlibris.com
Orders@Xlibris.com

ISBN:	Softcover	978-1-6641-2434-9
	EBook	978-1-6641-2433-2

Print information available on the last page

Rev. date: 09/09/2020

Dedicated to David P. Dilegge, 9 May 1956 - 2 May 2020

Dave Dilegge, founding Editor-in Chief of Small Wars Journal and a retired United States Marine Corps Reserve Intelligence and Counterintelligence officer served in Iraq during Operation Desert Storm earning a Combat Action Ribbon during an Iraqi counterattack on Burgan Oil Field and is widely considered the "grandfather of urban warfare studies."

TABLE OF CONTENTS

Contributors xviii

Prologue: COVID-19—Gangs, Statemaking, Threats, and Opportunities
       Steven Dudley xxv

Foreword: Pandemics and Conflict
       Nils Gilman.. xxx

Introduction: Pandemics, Governance, and Security
       John P. Sullivan and Robert J. Bunker xxxvi

Part 1: Strategic Notes

Chapter 1:   Third Generation Gangs Strategic Note No. 22: Rio's
               Gangs Impose Curfews in Response to Coronavirus
               John P. Sullivan, José de Arimatéia da Cruz and Robert J. Bunker............................1

Chapter 2:   Third Generation Gangs Strategic Note No. 23: El Salvadoran Gangs
               (Maras) Enforce Domestic Quarantine / Stay at Home Orders (Cuarentena domiciliar)
               John P. Sullivan, Robert J. Bunker and Juan Ricardo Gómez Hecht 11

Chapter 3:   Mexican Cartel Strategic Note No. 29: An Overview of
               Cartel Activities Related to COVID-19 Humanitarian Response
               Robert J. Bunker and John P. Sullivan 23

Chapter 4: Third Generation Gangs Strategic Note No. 24:
COVID-19, Gangs and Lockdown in Cape Town
John P. Sullivan and Robert J. Bunker 48

Chapter 5: Third Generation Gangs Strategic Note No. 26:
COVID-19, Revolutionaries and BACRIM in Colombia
Alexandra Phelan, John P. Sullivan and Robert J. Bunker 58

Chapter 6: Third Generation Gangs Strategic Note No. 27:
COVID-19 and Transnational Italian Mafias
Anna Sergi, John P. Sullivan and Robert J. Bunker 71

Part 2: Essays

Chapter 7: The Covid-19 Crisis and Future US National Security
Joseph J. Collins 86

Chapter 8: When pandemics come to slums
Vanda Felbab-Brown and Paul Wise 92

Chapter 9: Outbreak: COVID-19, Crime, and Conflict
Paul R. Kan 95

Chapter 10: Venezuela: Could the Coronavirus Threat Be an Opportunity
Keith Mines and Steven Hege 101

Chapter 11: The Coronavirus is a Call to Build Resilience in Fragile States
Nancy Lindborg 105

Chapter 12: Cyber-States and US National Security: Learning from Covid-19
Jonathan Lancelot 108

Chapter 13: Using Hybrid-Warfare Defeat Mechanisms to Fight the
Coronavirus and Counter Future Bioweapons. A Novel Approach
Justin Baumann 110

Part 3: Potentials

Conclusion: Gangs vs. States— The Battle Over the Contested Pandemic Space
    Robert J. Bunker and John P. Sullivan 118

Afterword: Terrorism, Biosecurity, and COVID-19
    Colin P. Clarke 124

Postscipt: Pandemics and Transnational Organized Crime
    Tuesday Reitano 129

Appendix 1: U.S. Naval War College—Humanitarian Response Program—Pandemic Response: Select Research & Game Findings 137

Selected Readings.. 151

ABOUT SMALL WARS JOURNAL AND FOUNDATION

Small Wars Journal facilitates the exchange of information among practitioners, thought leaders, and students of Small Wars, in order to advance knowledge and capabilities in the field. We hope this, in turn, advances the practice and effectiveness of those forces prosecuting Small Wars in the interest of self-determination, freedom, and prosperity for the population in the area of operations.

We believe that Small Wars are an enduring feature of modern politics. We do not believe that true effectiveness in Small Wars is a 'lesser included capability' of a force tailored for major theater war. And we *never* believed that 'bypass built-up areas' was a tenable position warranting the doctrinal primacy it has held for too long—this site is an evolution of the MOUT Homepage, Urban Operations Journal, and urbanoperations.com, all formerly run by the *Small Wars Journal's* founding Editor-in-Chief.

The characteristics of Small Wars have evolved since the Banana Wars and Gunboat Diplomacy. War is never purely military, but today's Small Wars are even less pure with the greater inter-connectedness of the 21st century. Their conduct typically involves the projection and employment of the full spectrum of national and coalition power by a broad community of practitioners. The military is still generally the biggest part of the pack, but there are a lot of other wolves. The strength of the pack is the wolf, and the strength of the wolf is the pack.

The *Small Wars Journal's* founders come from the Marine Corps. Like Marines deserve to be, we are very proud of this; we are also conscious and cautious of it. This site seeks to transcend any viewpoint that is single service, and any that is purely military or naively U.S.-centric. We pursue a comprehensive approach to Small Wars, integrating the full joint, allied, and coalition military with their governments' federal or national agencies, non-governmental agencies, and private organizations. Small Wars are big undertakings, demanding a coordinated effort from a huge community of interest.

We thank our contributors for sharing their knowledge and experience, and hope you will continue to join us as we build a resource for our community of interest to engage in a professional dialog on this painfully relevant topic. Share your thoughts, ideas, successes, and mistakes; make us all stronger.

"…I know it when I see it."

"Small Wars" is an imperfect term used to describe a broad spectrum of spirited continuation of politics by other means, falling somewhere in the middle bit of the continuum between feisty diplomatic words and global thermonuclear war. The *Small Wars Journal* embraces that imperfection.

Just as friendly fire isn't, there isn't necessarily anything small about a Small War.

The term "Small War" either encompasses or overlaps with a number of familiar terms such as counterinsurgency, foreign internal defense, support and stability operations, peacemaking, peacekeeping, and many flavors of intervention. Operations such as noncombatant evacuation, disaster relief, and humanitarian assistance will often either be a part of a Small War, or have a Small Wars feel to them. Small Wars involve a wide spectrum of specialized tactical, technical, social, and cultural skills and expertise, requiring great ingenuity from their practitioners. The *Small Wars Manual* (a wonderful resource, unfortunately more often referred to than read) notes that:

> *Small Wars demand the highest type of leadership directed by intelligence, resourcefulness, and ingenuity. Small Wars are conceived in uncertainty, are conducted often with precarious responsibility and doubtful authority, under indeterminate orders lacking specific instructions.*

The "three block war" construct employed by General Krulak is exceptionally useful in describing the tactical and operational challenges of a Small War and of many urban operations. Its only shortcoming is that is so useful that it is often mistaken as a definition or as a type of operation.

We'd like to deploy a primer on Small Wars that provides more depth than this brief section. Your suggestions and contributions of content are welcome.

Who Are Those Guys?

Small Wars Journal is NOT a government, official, or big corporate site. It is run by Small Wars Foundation, a non-profit corporation, for the benefit of the Small Wars community of interest. The site was founded by Dave Dilegge, its inaugural Editor-in-Chief. Its current principals are David S. Maxwell (Editor-in-Chief) and Bill Nagle (Publisher), and it would not be possible without the support of myriad volunteers as well as authors who care about this field and contribute their original works to the community. We do this in our spare time, because we want to. McDonald's pays more. But we'd rather work to advance our noble profession than watch TV, try to super-size your order, or interest you in a delicious hot apple pie. If and when you're not flipping burgers, please join us.

ABOUT EL CENTRO

El Centro is *SWJ's* focus on small wars in Latin America. The elephant in the hemispheric room is clearly the epidemic criminal, cartel and gang threat, fueled by a drug and migration economy, rising to the level of local and national criminal insurgencies and a significant U.S. national security risk. El Centro explores those and other issues across the US Southern Border Zone, Mexico, the Caribbean, Central and South America to develop a better understanding of the national and regional challenges underlying past, present, and future small wars.

The El Centro Main section presents relevant *Small Wars Journal* articles and *SWJ Blog* posts. Other sections have a reading list and research links of relevant external works. We do link to some Spanish language resources and occasionally put up an article in both Spanish and English, but we are pretty much mainly operating in English. We look forward to being able to roll out El Centro, en Español, dentro de poco.

The El Centro Fellows are a group of professionals with expertise in and commitment to the region who support *SWJ's* approach to advancing our field and have generously agreed to join us in our El Centro endeavor. With their help and with continued development on our site's news and library sections, we look forward to providing more El Centro-relevant *SWJ* original material and more useful access to other important works and resources in the future.

El Centro Fellows

The El Centro **Fellows** have expertise in and commitment to Latin America, support SWJ's particular focus on the small wars in the region, and agree with SWJ's general approach to advancing discussion and awareness in the field through community dialog and publishing.

El Centro **Associates** are actively engaged in research or practice in the region and in transnational organized crime or insurgency. The **Fellows** have already made significant and distinguished contributions to the field through the course of their career. The **Senior Fellows** are Fellows that are central to producing SWJ El Centro and are very active in managing our work in this focus area.

Senior Fellows

- Robert J. Bunker
- John P. Sullivan

Fellows

- Michael L. Burgoyne
- Edgardo Buscaglia
- Irina A. Chindea
- José de Arimatéia da Cruz
- Steven S. Dudley
- Douglas Farah
- Vanda Felbab-Brown
- Luis Jorge Garay-Salamanca
- Ioan Grillo

- Gary J. Hale
- Nathan P. Jones
- Paul Rexton Kan
- Robert Killebrew
- Max G. Manwaring
- Molly Molloy
- Robert Muggah
- Luz E. Nagle
- Eduardo Salcedo-Albarán
- Robert H. Scales

Associates

- Pamela Ligouri Bunker
- Alma Keshavarz
- Marisa Mendoza

Interns

- Anibal Serrano
- Angelo Thomas

Past Fellows

- George W. Grayson
- Graham H. Turbiville, Jr.

The views expressed in this reader are those of the author(s) and do not necessarily reflect the official policy or position of the Department of the Army, the Department of Defense, the Federal Bureau of Investigation, the Department of Justice, or the U.S. Government, or any other U.S. armed service, intelligence or law enforcement agency, or local or state government.

CONTRIBUTORS

Editors

Dr. Robert J. Bunker is Director of Research and Analysis, C/O Futures, LLC, and an adjunct research professor, Strategic Studies Institute, US Army War College. He holds university degrees in political science, government, social science, anthropology-geography, behavioral science, and history and has undertaken hundreds of hours of counterterrorism training. Past professional associations include Minerva Chair at the Strategic Studies Institute, U.S. Army War College and Futurist in Residence, Training and Development Division, Behavioral Science Unit, Federal Bureau of Investigation Academy, Quantico. He has well over 500 publications—including about 40 books as co-author, editor, and co-editor—and can be reached at docbunker@smallwarsjournal.com.

Dr. John P. Sullivan was a career police officer. He is an honorably retired lieutenant with the Los Angeles Sheriff's Department, specializing in emergency operations, transit policing, counterterrorism, and intelligence. He is currently an Instructor in the Safe Communities Institute (SCI) at the Sol Price School of Public Policy, University of Southern California. Sullivan received a lifetime achievement award from the National Fusion Center Association in November 2018 for his contributions to the national network of intelligence fusion centers. He completed the CREATE Executive Program in Counter-Terrorism at the University of Southern California and holds a Bachelor of Arts in Government from the College of William and Mary, a Master of Arts in Urban Affairs and Policy Analysis from the New School for Social Research, and a PhD from the Open University of Catalonia (Universitat Oberta de Catalunya). His doctoral thesis was "Mexico's Drug War: Cartels, Gangs, Sovereignty and the Network State." He can be reached at jpsullivan@smallwarsjournal.com.

Contributors

Justin Baumann is a U.S. Army Officer. He has a B.A. in History and German from the University of Portland (Oregon), and a Masters of Public Administration from the University of Southern California (USC). He has previously deployed to Afghanistan and Iraq.

Dr. Colin P. Clarke is a teaching professor in the Institute for Politics and Strategy (IPS) at Carnegie Mellon University, where he also has responsibilities with the Institute for Strategic Analysis (ISA) and serves on the executive board for the Masters of Information Technology Strategy (MITS) program. Before coming to CMU, Clarke spent nearly a decade at the RAND Corporation where he was a senior political scientist focusing on terrorism, insurgency, and criminal networks. At RAND, Clarke directed studies on ISIS financing, the future of terrorism and transnational crime, and lessons learned from all insurgencies between the end of WWII and 2009. He was also a member of the Pardee RAND Graduate School (PRGS) faculty. He is also an associate fellow at the International Centre for Counter-Terrorism–The Hague (ICCT), a non-resident Senior Fellow at the Foreign Policy Research Institute (FPRI), and a member of the network of experts at the Global Initiative Against Transnational Organized Crime. He was previously a fellow at the Program on Extremism at George Washington University and the Matthew B. Ridgway Center for International Security Studies at the University of Pittsburgh's Graduate School of Public and International Affairs (GSPIA), where he received his Ph.D. in international security policy (2012).

Dr. Joseph J. Collins, a retired Army Colonel, served DoD in and out of uniform for four decades. His decade plus in the Pentagon was capped off by service as Deputy Assistant Secretary of Defense for Stability Operations, 2001-04. He taught for 25 years at West Point and the National War College, and for more than two decades in Georgetown University's Security Studies Program. He is an author in and co-editor (with Richard Hooker) of *Lessons Encountered: Learning from the Long War*, NDU Press, 2015. Collins is a life member of the Council on Foreign Relations and holds a doctorate in Political Science from Columbia University.

Dr. José de Arimatéia da Cruz is a Professor of International Relations and International Studies at Georgia Southern University, Savannah, GA. He also is an Adjunct Research Professor at the U.S. Army War College, Strategic Studies Institute, Carlisle, PA, and a Research Fellow of the Brazil Research Unit at the Council on Hemispheric Affairs in Washington, DC. He is also a SWJ El Centro Fellow.

Steven Dudley is the co-founder and co-director of *InSight Crime*, and a senior fellow at American University's Center for Latin American and Latino Studies in Washington, D.C. He is the former Bureau Chief of *The Miami Herald* in the Andean Region and the author of *Walking Ghosts: Murder and Guerrilla Politics in Colombia* (Routledge 2004). Dudley has also reported from Haiti, Brazil, Nicaragua, Cuba and Miami for National Public Radio and The Washington Post, among others. Dudley has a B.A. in Latin American History from Cornell University and an M.A. in Latin American Studies from the University of Texas at Austin. He was awarded the Knight Fellowship at Stanford University in 2007, and is a member of the International Consortium of Investigative Journalists. In 2012 to 2013, he was a visiting fellow at the Woodrow Wilson International Center for Scholars. His second book, *MS-13: The Making of the World's Most Notorious Gang* (HarperCollins), will be published in September 2020. He is also a SWJ El Centro Fellow.

Dr. Vanda Felbab-Brown is a senior fellow in the Center for 21st Century Security and Intelligence in the Foreign Policy program at Brookings. She is also the director of the Brookings project, "Improving Global Drug Policy: Comparative Perspectives Beyond UNGASS 2016," and co-director of another Brookings project, "Reconstituting Local Orders." Felbab-Brown is an expert on international and internal conflicts and nontraditional security threats, including insurgency, organized crime, urban violence, and illicit economies. Her fieldwork and research have covered, among others, Afghanistan, South Asia, Burma, Indonesia, the Andean region, Mexico, Morocco, Somalia, and eastern Africa. She is a senior advisor to the congressionally mandated Afghanistan Peace Process Study Group. She is also a SWJ El Centro Fellow.

Dr. Nils Gilman is Vice President of Programs at the Berggruen Institute. From 2013 to 2017 he served as Associate Chancellor and Chief of Staff to the Chancellor at U.C. Berkeley, and as the Founding Executive Director of Social Science Matrix, Berkeley's flagship interdisciplinary social science research center. Earlier in this career, he worked as a research director and scenario planning consultant at the Monitor Group and Global Business Network, and in software companies such as Salesforce.com and BEA Systems. He is the author of *Mandarins of the Future: Modernization Theory in Cold War America* (2004), *Deviant Globalization: Black Market Economy in the 21st Century* (2011), the Sidney Award-winning essay, "The Twin Insurgency," (*The American Interest,* 2014) as well as numerous other articles on intellectual history and political economy. He holds a B.A., M.A., and Ph.D. in History from U.C. Berkeley.

Juan Ricardo Gómez Hecht, works as Professor at the College of Advanced Strategic Studies, the Highest Post Graduate School of El Salvador's Armed Forces. Previously he served 16 years in the area of public security, holding various important positions within the General Inspectorate of the National Civilian Police of El Salvador. Academically he is a political scientist and holds two Master's degrees: in Public Administration and Human Rights and Education for Peace (University of El Salvador. Currently he is a candidate for the degree of Doctor of Philosophy. Prof. Gómez Hecht has a teaching experience that spans 19 years at graduate and post graduate level at various El Salvador Universities, National Public Security Academy and most Officer Schools of the Armed Forces. He is an Academic researcher accredited by the Council for Science and Technology of El Salvador and has published works in national and international specialized journals in the United States, Spain, Colombia and Nicaragua. He has also lectured on defense and security issues at the national level and in the United States, Mexico, Morocco, Chile, Colombia, Guatemala, Nicaragua and Panama.

Steven Hege has nearly two decades of professional experience working on issues related to peace processes, human rights, security sector reform, local governance, and natural resource-related organized crime. He currently leads USIP's efforts in Colombia in support of the implementation of the peace accord with the FARC rebels, the dialogues with the ELN, as well as local peacebuilding and security transformations in municipalities previously under rebel control or influence. Additionally, Steve serves as an advisor in the peace process in Myanmar providing technical assistance to ethnic armed groups and political parties on security structure design and the merging of non-state actors with government institutions. Over the last four years, he has also supported or managed USIP security and justice reform programs in the Democratic Republic of the Congo (DRC), Tanzania, Central African Republic, Myanmar and Colombia.

Dr. Paul R. Kan is currently Professor of National Security Studies at the US Army War College. He is also the author of the books *Drugs and Contemporary Warfare* (Potomac Books, 2009) and *Cartels at War: Mexico's Drug Fueled Violence and the Threat to US National Security* (Potomac Books, 2012). His most recent book is *Drug Trafficking and International Security* (Rowman and Littlefield, 2016). In 2011, he was the Senior Visiting Counternarcotics Advisor with ISAF in Kabul, Afghanistan. He is also a SWJ El Centro Fellow.

Jonathan Lancelot is an independent Foreign and Cyber Policy Advisor at CyberDetente LLC, where Jonathan leads in consulting organizations on cybersecurity risk management, including advising on the geopolitical implications of cyberspace on US foreign policy and build cyber organizational systems. His research interests are in blockchain technology, Lex Cryptographica, and how it will affect governance in the future. Jonathan graduated from Norwich University with a Master's in Diplomacy with a sharp focus on cyber-diplomacy, and published the widely shared paper "Russia Today, Cyberterrorists Tomorrow: US Failure to Prepare Democracy for Cyberspace," with is published on Embry-Riddle Aeronautical University's *Journal of Digital Forensic, Security and Law*, and a contributor at *Small Wars Journal*. Jonathan also is an experienced computer technician that was trained and certified by Apple engineers and worked at the US Senate and the Department of Defense.

Nancy Lindborg has served as the president and CEO of the U.S. Institute of Peace since February 2015. Created by Congress in 1984 as an independent, nonpartisan, federally funded institute to prevent, mitigate, and resolve violent conflict around the world, USIP links research, policy, training and direct action with partners in conflict-affected areas. Prior to joining USIP, she served as the assistant administrator for the Bureau for Democracy, Conflict and Humanitarian Assistance (DCHA) at USAID. From 2010 through 2014, Ms. Lindborg directed the efforts of more than 600 team members in nine offices focused on crisis prevention, response, recovery and transition. She also led response teams for some of the biggest challenges the world was facing at the time, including the crisis in Syria, the droughts in the Sahel and the Horn of Africa, the Arab Spring, as well as the Ebola crisis. Ms. Lindborg has spent most of her career working on issues of transition, democracy and civil society, conflict and humanitarian response. Prior to joining USAID, she was president of Mercy Corps, where she spent 14 years helping to grow the organization into a globally respected organization known for innovative programs in the most challenging environments. She previously lived and worked in Nepal and Central Asia. She was a founding member of the National Committee for North Korea and served as co-chair of the board of the US Global Leadership Coalition. She holds a B.A. and an M.A. in English literature from Stanford University and an M.A. in public administration from the John F. Kennedy School of Government at Harvard University.

Keith Mines is a senior advisor for Colombia and Venezuela in USIP's Applied Conflict Transformation Center. Mr. Mines joined USIP after a career at the State Department, where he was most recently director for Andean and Venezuelan affairs. In 32 years of diplomatic and military service, he has worked on governance and institution building in Central America; Middle East peace in Israel and the West Bank; post-conflict stabilization in Haiti, Iraq, and Afghanistan; global financial stability and the environment in Brazil; NATO expansion in Hungary; famine relief and tribal reconciliation in Darfur and Somali; and creating a culture of lawfulness as the first director of the Merida Initiative in Mexico City.

Dr. Alexandra Phelan is a Lecturer in Politics and International Relations at Monash University, and Deputy Director of the Monash Gender, Peace and Security Centre (Monash GPS) in Victoria, Australia.

Her research focuses on insurgent governance, and her PhD examined why the Colombian government shifted between counterinsurgency and negotiation with FARC from 1982-2016. Based on an extensive examination of primary FARC material, and interviews with former and active FARC, ELN, M-19 and AUC members, she examined how insurgent legitimation activities shaped government response.

Tuesday Reitano is the Deputy Director of the Global Initiative Against Transnational Organized Crime (www.globalinitiative.net) a global network dedicated to countering transnational organized crime. She holds three Master's degrees: one in Business Administration (MBA) from McGill University, another in Public Administration (MPA) from New York University, and a master's in Security, Conflict and International Development (MSc) from Leicester University. She previously lead a policy and monitoring body for the EU's engagements in countering terrorism, and worked for 12 years in the UN System as a policy specialist in transnational organized crime and fragile states.

Dr. Anna Sergi holds a PhD in Sociology (2014), with specialisation in Criminology, from the Department of Sociology at the University of Essex, where she has worked since 2015 as Senior Lecturer. Her research specialism is in organised crime studies and comparative criminal justice. She has published extensively in renowned peer-review journals on topics related to Italian mafias both in Italy and abroad as well as on policing strategies against organised crime across states. She has authored three monographs on these topics.

Dr. Paul Wise is the Richard E. Behrman Professor of Child Health and Society and Professor of Pediatrics and Health Policy at Stanford University School of Medicine. Dr. Wise is also a Senior Fellow in the Center for Democracy, Development and the Rule of Law and the Center for International Security and Cooperation, in the Freeman-Spogli Institute for International Studies, Stanford University. He is also co-Director of the March of Dimes Center for Prematurity Research at Stanford University. Dr. Wise received his A.B. degree *summa cum laude* in Latin American Studies and his M.D. degree from Cornell University, a Master of Public Health degree from the Harvard School of Public Health and did his pediatric training at the Children's Hospital in Boston. His former positions include Director of Emergency and Primary Care Services at Boston Children's Hospital, Director of the Harvard Institute for Reproductive and Child Health, and Vice-Chief of the Division of Social Medicine and Health Inequalities at the Brigham and Women's Hospital and Harvard Medical School. He served as Special Assistant to the U.S. Surgeon General, Chair of the Steering Committee of the NIH Global Network for Women's and Children's Health

Research, and currently is a member of the Advisory Council of the National Institute of Child Health and Human Development, NIH. Dr. Wise's research focuses on health inequalities, child health policy, and global child health. He leads a multidisciplinary initiative, Children in Crisis, which is directed at integrating expertise in political science, security, and health services in areas of civil conflict and unstable governance.

Prologue:

COVID-19—Gangs, Statemaking, Threats, and Opportunities

Steven Dudley

Washington, District of Columbia

2 July 2020

It was March 2020, not long after fear of the coronavirus began spreading across the Americas, when several major criminal groups started employing their own form of a lockdown.

In Brazil, the *Comando Vermelho* (Red Command), the vaunted prison gang, began issuing stay-at-home orders via social media.

"Stay home," one tweet said. "This thing is getting serious."

In El Salvador, street gangs were enforcing a curfew issued by the government in the poor neighborhoods they controlled.[1] In Colombia, current and former guerrillas threatened citizens who defied the strict government lockdown in rural areas.[2] And in Venezuela, paramilitaries in Caracas shantytowns worked with government shock troops to keep people indoors.[3]

Charles Tilly once famously described "war risking and state making" as "our largest examples of organized crime," and proffered the idea that criminal groups helped create the modern-day nation state.[4] Now, with the onset of coronavirus, we can add a corollary: Criminal groups may help *maintain* the modern-day nation state.

Mitigating the spread of coronavirus is only the beginning. Over time, the virus is sure to wipe out thousands of businesses, leave millions unemployed, and destroy 30 years of progress against poverty in the region. Governments, bereft of tax revenue and other forms of traditional financial sources, will be hard-pressed to keep police and military on the streets for long periods of time, much less regulate the booming informal economies that will surface.

With coronavirus, there will not be one Tri-Border Area (TBA)—the infamous region encompassing parts of Brazil, Paraguay and Argentina that bustles with sales of illegal medicine, knock-off clothing and electronics, contraband cigarettes and high-powered assault rifles—but a dozen TBAs. What's more, the neoliberal model, dependent on open borders and free-wheeling travel, will be hobbled for years. Whatever temporary or permanent system replaces it will take some time to emerge.

In the interim, there will be criminal governance. At bare minimum, these criminals will provide handouts. Early during the pandemic in Mexico, splinter groups from the Gulf Cartel illustrated how this will work when they handed out boxes of rice and beans,[5] while the Jalisco Cartel New Generation (*Cartel de Jalisco Nueva Generación* – CJNG) provided people with cooking oil, bread, jam and toilet paper.[6] In Rio de Janeiro, the gangs were passing out soap.[7]

But mostly, criminal groups will become *de facto* regulators of commercial, political and social transactions that govern the day-to-day lives of people. In some instances, that may be benign. In Brazil, prison gangs threatened potential price gougers.[8] In Guatemala, the 18th Street gang temporarily suspended the practice of collecting extortion in at least one neighborhood.[9] However, in other instances, they will be predatory, such as the case of the *La Unión Tepito* criminal group in Mexico City, which threatened merchants who did not pay their weekly quota to the group.[10]

This dichotomy is not new, of course. The state, as Tilly noted, needed these criminals to instill peace where it had no presence and enforce social order where it had little or no legitimacy, even when it meant leaving these areas to the whims of predatory criminal groups. "Banditry, piracy, gangland rivalry, policing and war making all belong on the same continuum," he wrote.[11]

Such is the situation with COVID-19 where the social contract will be enforced by a lethal stew of state and non-state actors who may not only determine whether people can purchase food on any given day but also where their children go to school, whether they will get health care, and if they can attend church. As the Brookings Institute's Vanda Felbab-Brown once wrote, "It is thus important to stop thinking about crime solely as aberrant social activity to be suppressed, but instead think of crime as a competition in state-making."[12]

What's more, life during and immediately following the pandemic promises to be hyper-local, as does this criminal governance. And the most powerful groups will have both a physical and metaphysical presence. They will control physical territory where semi-independent cells exert control with a never-ending supply of recruits, all the more so with the destruction of the economy and the temporary halt of schools.[13]

But they will also control a metaphysical space. In this regard, prison gangs appear especially well-positioned to take advantage of the virus. Prison gangs have flourished throughout the Americas in the last 20 years, especially where governments have packed penitentiaries far above capacity then abdicated their power to them. And as one of the most likely vectors for illness, prisons are even more ripe for alternative governance—as well as violent backlash—in the face of the State's incompetence or a misguided ideological approach to the pandemic.

What's more, with the pandemic, criminal economies—many of which already flow through prisons—will now mirror them. As the formal economy collapses and supply chains falter, improvisation amidst shortages will become a way of life, informal markets will surge along with the informal forms of securing loans and other capital. In this environment, prison gangs—who already thrive in these quarantine conditions moving contraband in tight spaces under strict guard—will flourish. The state crackdowns that are sure to follow the emergence of new, informal markets and the loansharking that accompanies them will only fortify this system and the ethos they have built up around it.

States and political parties will face little choice but to forge formal and informal alliances with groups that help them keep their shaky social contract afloat. As Juan Belikow, who has worked on citizen security issues with the World Bank and the Organization of American States, noted in an essay published after the pandemic began, these alliances are part a "perverse symbiosis of great mutual benefit between delinquency and politics."[14]

This had already happened to a great extent inside the prisons prior to the pandemic. With coronavirus, it promises to extend to both urban and rural areas, especially where traditional economic activity collapses and the virus exposes just how dysfunctional, corrupt or absent these states and political proxies are.

Not coincidentally, governments under the most strain were the first to seek what can be called a criminal equilibrium. This included Brazil, where there was immediate talk of releasing prisoners early. Almost waving a white flag, the health later minister later suggested the government hold talks with criminal groups in the *favelas*.

"We have to understand that these are areas where the state is often absent and the ones in charge are drug traffickers and militia groups," the minister said at a news conference.[15]

The words echoed Tilly's own: "The analogy between war making and state making, on the one hand, and organized crime, on the other, is becoming tragically apt."[16]

Endnotes

[1] Parker Asmann, "What Does Coronavirus Mean for Criminal Governance in Latin America?" *InSight Crime*. 31 March 2020, https://www.insightcrime.org/news/analysis/criminal-governance-latin-america-coronavirus/.

[2] Ibid.

[3] Ibid.

[4] Charles Tilly, "War Making and State Making as Organized Crime," in Peter Evans, Dietrich Rueschemer and Theda Skocpol, Eds. *Bringing the State Back*. Cambridge: Cambridge University Press, 1991. pp. 169-191.

[5] Juan Alberto Cedillo, "El Cartel del Golfo reparte despensas en Tamaulipas por covid-19." *Proceso*. 6 April 2020, https://www.proceso.com.mx/624665/el-cartel-del-golfo-reparte-despensas-en-tamaulipas-por-covid-19.

[6] "CJNG reparte despensas para ayudar a familias en tiempos del coronavirus." *La Opinión*.15 April 2020, https://laopinion.com/2020/04/15/cjng-reparte-despensas-para-ayudar-a-familias-en-tiempos-del-coronavirus/.

[7] Caio Barretto Briso and Tom Phillips, "Brazil gangs impose strict curfews to slow coronavirus spread." *The Guardian*. 25 March 2020, https://amp.theguardian.com/world/2020/mar/25/brazil-rio-gangs-coronavirus.

[8] Leslie Leitão e Marco Antônio Martins, "Traficantes ameaçam comércio em favelas do Rio contra o aumento de preço do álcool gel." *G1*. 26 March 2020, https://g1.globo.com/rj/rio-de-janeiro/noticia/2020/03/26/traficantes-ameacam-comercio-em-favelas-do-rio-contra-o-aumento-de-preco-do-alcool-gel.ghtml.

[9] R. Ríos y L. Sapalú, "Pandilleros conceden indulto en el cobro de extorsión," *elPeriódico (de Guatemala)*. 26 March 2020, https://elperiodico.com.gt/nacion/2020/03/26/pandilleros-conceden-indulto-en-el-cobro-de-extorsion/.

[10] Maria Alejandra Navarrete, "Coronavirus Affects Extortion Payments in Mexico and Central America." *InSight Crime*. 13 April 2020, https://www.insightcrime.org/news/analysis/coronavirus-extortion-mexico-central-america/.

[11] Tilly, op cit. (at Note 4).

[12] Vanda Felbab-Brown, "Conceptualizing Crime as Competition in State-Making and Designing an Effective Response," from a speech given to the *Conference on Illicit Trafficking Activities in the Western Hemisphere: Possible Strategies and Lessons Learned*. Washington, DC: Brookings Institution. 21 May 2010, https://www.brookings.edu/on-the-record/conceptualizing-crime-as-competition-in-state-making-and-designing-an-effective-response/.

[13] Lara Loaiza, "Armed Groups in Colombia Target Children Amid Pandemic." *InSight Crime*. 22 June 2020, https://www.insightcrime.org/news/brief/coronavirus-recruitment-minors-colombia/.

[14] Juan Belikow, "El crimen organizado en la post-pandemia." *Infobae*. 3 June 2020, https://www.infobae.com/america/opinion/2020/06/03/el-crimen-organizado-en-la-post-pandemia/.

[15] "Brazil minister wants talks with narcos on coronavirus." Agence France Presse. 9 April 2020, https://www.rappler.com/world/regions/latin-america/257461-brazil-minister-talks-narcos-coronavirus.

[16] Tilly, op cit. (at Note 4).

Foreword

Pandemics and Conflict

Nils Gilman

Los Angeles and San Francisco, California

30 June 2020

The Covid-19 pandemic is remaking the political economy of the illicit, the underground, and the antinomian as inexorably as it is the legal, aboveboard, and mainstream landscape. In brief, the pandemic has had four main effects on "deviant" political economy, effects that are likely to long outlast the immediate impact of the disease itself. First, it has disrupted certain deviant supply chains; second, it has created opportunity/demand for others; third, the inadequacies of the response to the pandemic are accelerating the fragmentation and delegitimation of local, national, global governance institutions; and finally, the vacuum created by failing mainstream institutions is accelerating the emergence of "alt-governance" actors (including some from the criminal sector) who are providing humanitarian and social assistance where governments are failing to do so.

One immediate effect of the pandemic has been the collapse in international movement of goods and people, which has disrupted existing deviant supply chains just as it has licit ones. For example, the farmhouse gate price of coca in Peru and Ecuador is reported to have dropped by almost three quarters, as border lockdowns have disrupted the ability to move product as well as to acquire chemicals needed for processing, even as street prices of the drug have climbed in Europe and United States. Meanwhile, "In Afghanistan, virus lockdowns have created acute shortages of lancers — the specialized workers, many from neighboring Pakistan, who cut the seedpods of mature poppies to produce heroin."[1]

Pandemic-induced supply chain disruptions are no mere temporary blip, but are instead likely to produce long term reconfiguration of many illicit industries. As with licit business, "the largest [illicit] operators are positioned to weather the storm far better than smaller competitors," the long-term effect is likely to be market "consolidation as labor and smugglers defect to or are recruited by the strongest players." Michael S. Vigil, former chief of international operations for the DEA, explained to the *Washington Post* that, "This will change the landscape of these cartels. The only ones that may survive are the supersized cartels. They'll completely obliterate the smaller ones that don't have the infrastructure or revenue streams to survive the supply chain disruption we're seeing now."[2]

The disruption of existing supply chains, both licit and illicit, is also encouraging deviant entrepreneurs to develop new deviant markets and supply chains. One effect, for example, is the rise of substitute illicit goods. For example, there is some evidence that the collapse of global cocaine supply chains is spurring the rise of demand for methamphetamine, which can be produced synthetically for local markets.[3] The collapse of licit supply chains has also encouraged the rise of deviant substitutes. For example, in Africa, legal diamond exports have almost completely collapsed, and globally diamond prices have dropped by half or more. According to the Kimberly Process Civil Society Coalition, an industry watchdog, "there are reports of opportunistic and criminal actors stepping into this void, luring desperate miners into exploitative sponsor deals that force them to sell production at drastically reduced prices.… illicit actors may be stocking up on cheap artisanal diamonds, which they hope to sell with huge profits when the disruptions of international supply chains will be relaxed. There are indications that ill-intentioned actors are quickly finding new money-making opportunities amidst this crisis. In Zimbabwe for instance, the closure of official border posts is said to be leading to an increase of diamond smuggling to Mozambique via illegal exit points."[4]

Likewise, in South Africa, coronavirus-related bans of alcohol and cigarettes "have created a booming illicit trade, providing huge opportunities for organized criminals. Police have described an increase in smuggling of contraband into South Africa from its neighbors and a spate of burglaries of stores stocking alcohol." As Gareth Newham, head of the governance, crime and justice division at the Institute for Security Studies, a think tank in Pretoria, told *The Guardian*, "This has given a massive boost to organized crime. Demand has remained the same, but the supply side has simply shifted into the control of the illicit industry. It is going to be very difficult to roll back."[5] Similar "marketing darkening" reconfigurations are surely taking for everything from Siberian timber to Burmese sapphires to South African abalone—whose lucrative global markets have always had both licit and black dimensions.[6]

In addition, the pandemic is spurring various kinds of deviant innovation. The pandemic has, for example, occasioned an explosion of Covid-19 related "scam" sites, ranging from fake offers of tax rebates to bogus medicines.[7] In May 2020, the European Anti-Fraud Office announced that they had already identified 340 companies trading in counterfeit products linked to the pandemic.[8] In the United States, Customs and Border Patrol has been seizing hundreds of thousands of unapproved test kits, unproven medicines and substandard protective equipment.[9] In addition, the shift of many knowledge workers to working from home has multiplied the vulnerabilities that hackers can use to exploit companies' systems.[10] Russian hackers in particular appear to be targeting US workers at home.[11] Such attacks are increasing the threat from ransomware (malware that can lock computer files and open them only on payment of a ransom): in one June 2020 case, Covid-19 researchers at the University of California San Francisco School of Medicine were the victim of such a ransomware attack, and were forced to pay over a million dollars to liberate their data.[12] Certainly for deviant actors, every crisis is an opportunity.

Beyond the immediate criminogenic effects of the pandemic, the bungled response of many governments to the pandemic is accelerating the fragmentation and delegitimation of local, national, global governance institutions. One reason why organized crime has been able to effectively respond to the pandemic is that, as the Guardian recently observed, "the resources of the state, including the police, are being diverted to cope with the consequences of the disease. While officers are busy stopping members of the public from congregating in parks, they have less time to track down criminals."[13] Despite often diverting government resources into addressing the pandemic, governments across the globe and of every ideological stripe have failed to contain the virus. The worst results have come in countries run by "anti-globalist" populist strongmen, such as Donald Trump's United States, which by early July 2020 had experienced over 130,000 deaths; Jair Bolsonaro's Brazil, with over 60,000 deaths; and Boris Johnson's United Kingdom, with over 43,000. These leaders lack of (indeed contempt for) basic operational competence has been directly responsible for the catastrophe that has unfolded on their watch.[14] Rather than delegitimating anti-globalism, however, the virus is only furthering the drive to deglobalization, even though this only makes containing a global pandemic more difficult.[15]

This void in credible, competence governance by the state has in turn accelerated the emergence of "alt-governance" actors (including some from the criminal sector) who are providing humanitarian and social assistance where governments are failing to do so. As the *Guardian* observes, "In countries where the state is weak and unable to provide essential goods and services to distressed communities, organised crime will step into the vacuum."[16] For example, from Rio to Central America, gangs are imposing curfews, enforcing social distancing, and handing out medicine.[17] As Sullivan and Bunker argue in their contribution to this volume, the gangs "are acting in the manner of social bandits as describes by Hobsbawn and later by Sullivan in the context of criminal insurgents." One can only assume that where the government fails and gangs succeed in providing useful social services, primary political loyalties will surely shift accordingly.

In short, the pandemic has, at least in its initial phases, been a boon to criminals and a disaster for states, particularly Western ones that have signaling failed to contain the virus. But perhaps all is not lost. The hopeful view, put forward in different registers both by Keith Mines and Steven Hege in their account of the pandemic Venezuela and by Nancy Linborg in her "call to build resilience in fragile states," is the inadequacies in local, national, and global governance that the pandemic has exposed will provide and prompt and impetus for re-integrating development with policing. Doing so would allow policy to move beyond the 20th century model of policing-as-punitive-counterinsurgency, which seeks to contain and isolate criminal elements, rather than address the socio-economic causes of criminality at their root.[18] In the end, we can hope that the lessons that will be drawn from the pandemic will be to reinvest in the operational competence of the states, resocialize collective risks, and above all to take a longer-term view of the threat environment.[19]

Endnotes

[1] Anthony Faiola and Lucien Chauvin, "The coronavirus has gutted the price of coca. It could reshape the cocaine trade." *Washington Post*. 9 June 2020, https://www.washingtonpost.com/world/the_americas/coronavirus-coca-crash-bolivia-colombia-peru-latin-america/2020/06/09/8c7da42c-a11f-11ea-be06-af5514ee0385_story.html.

[2] Ibid.

[3] Ian Hamilton and Harry Sumnall, "Crystal meth: Europe could now see a surge in supply and use." *The Conversation*. 15 June 2020, https://theconversation.com/crystal-meth-europe-could-now-see-a-surge-in-supply-and-use-140606.

[4] "The Impact of COVID-19 on African communities affected by diamond mining." Kimberly Process Civil Society Coalition, June 2020, https://www.kpcivilsociety.org/report/the-impact-of-covid-19-on-african-communities-affected-by-diamond-mining/.

[5] Jason Burke, "South Africa's alcohol ban has given 'massive boost' to criminal gangs." *The Guardian*. 31 May 2020, https://www.theguardian.com/world/2020/may/31/south-africas-alcohol-ban-has-given-massive-boost-to-criminal-gangs.

[6] See Nils Gilman, Jesse Goldhammer, Steven Weber, Eds., *Deviant Globalization: Black Market Economy in the 21st Century*. New York: Continuum Books, 2012. On abalone, see also Kimon de Greef, "South Africa's Abalone Black Market Is Being Squeezed by COVID-19." *Hakai Magazine*. 21 May 2020, https://www.hakaimagazine.com/news/south-africas-abalone-black-market-is-being-squeezed-by-covid-19/.

[7] Paul Lynch, "Criminals prey on coronavirus fears to steal £2m." *BBC News*. 16 April 2020, https://www.bbc.com/news/uk-england-52310804.

[8] "Inquiry into fake COVID-19 products progresses." European Anti-Fraud Office, 13 May 2020, https://ec.europa.eu/anti-fraud/media-corner/news/13-05-2020/inquiry-fake-covid-19-products-progresses_en.

[9] Aaron Boyd, "Customs officers have picked up hundreds of thousands of unapproved test kits, unproven medicines and substandard protective equipment." *Nextgov*. 5 June 2020, https://www.nextgov.com/cio-briefing/2020/06/cbp-has-seized-nearly-900000-counterfeit-and-unsafe-covid-19-supplies/165959/.

[10] Felipe Erazo, "Researchers Say Ransomware Attacks on the Rise as More People Work From Home." *Cointelegraph*. 29 June 2020, https://cointelegraph.com/news/researchers-say-ransomware-attacks-on-the-rise-as-more-people-work-from-home.

[11] "Russian hacker group Evil Corp targets US workers at home." *BBC News*. 26 June 2020, https://www.bbc.com/news/world-us-canada-53195749.

[12] Davey Winder, "The University Of California Pays $1 Million Ransom Following Cyber Attack." *Forbes*. 29 June 2020, https://www.forbes.com/sites/daveywinder/2020/06/29/the-university-of-california-pays-1-million-ransom-following-cyber-attack/#12db7da718a8.

[13] Misha Glenny, "From drug dealers to loan sharks: how coronavirus empowers organised crime." *The Guardian*. 7 June 2020, https://www.theguardian.com/commentisfree/2020/jun/07/drug-dealers-loan-sharks-organised-crime-coronavirus.

[14] James Fallows, "The 3 Weeks That Changed Everything." *The Atlantic*. 29 June 2020, https://www.theatlantic.com/politics/archive/2020/06/how-white-house-coronavirus-response-went-wrong/613591/.

[15] Bryan Walsh, "The coronavirus is a force for deglobalization." *Axios*. 20 May 2020, https://www.axios.com/coronavirus-economic-globalization-744b0660-ce56-4ffa-93e9-cc4c20ee135c.html.

[16] Misha Glenny, "From drug dealers to loan sharks: how coronavirus empowers organised crime." Note 13.

[17] Sam Hall, "Drug gangs in Brazil hand out medication and enforce social distancing instead of government." *iNews*. 14 June 2020, https://inews.co.uk/news/world/coronavirus-drug-gangs-brazil-hand-out-medication-enforce-social-distancing-government-445979.

[18] Nils Gilman, "SWJ Book Review: The Chickens of Empire Come Home to Roost - Badges without Borders: How Global Counterinsurgency Transformed American Policing." *Small Wars Journal*. 12 April 2020, https://smallwarsjournal.com/jrnl/art/swj-book-review-chickens-empire-come-home-roost-badges-without-borders-how-global.

[19] Steven Weber and Nils Gilman, "The Long Shadow Of The Future." *Noēma Magazine*. June 2020, https://www.noemamag.com/the-long-shadow-of-the-future/.

Introduction

Pandemics, Governance, and Security

John P. Sullivan and Robert J. Bunker

Los Angeles, California

8 July 2020

This edited collection looks at the influence of the COVID-19 pandemic on gangs and conflict. Specifically, it looks at how the pandemic has created opportunities and challenges for states and organized criminal groups (OCGs), including criminal armed groups (CAGs) such as gangs, militias, and mafias. The contributors represent a cross section of security professionals and scholars engaged in pandemic planning, response, and forecasting activities as they relate to gang and OCG impacts and futures as well as state governance and political capacity issues.

Conflict Potentials

The COVID-19 pandemic is not only a significant global public health emergency, but also a significant geopolitical event challenging governance at all levels. From a public health perspective, the severe acute respiratory syndrome (SARS) outbreak is caused by a novel coronavirus known as SARS-CoV-2. The outbreak is known as COVID-19 because it is a **co**rona **vi**rus **d**isease initially reported in Wuhan, China in 20**19**. This global pandemic has inflamed political passions from all vantage points. On the right (and also on the extreme left, leading to a convergence of antigovernment action), militia and antigovernment groups in the United States have rejected public health initiatives including lockdowns, quarantines, stay at home orders, and mandatory mask requirements as an affront to their view of individual liberties.[1][2]

The COVID-19 pandemic and subsequent political rejection of public safety measures and/or lack of state capacity to address the pandemic by some states contribute to global conflict potentials in range of situations. Humanitarian aid flows are disrupted and peace operations and peacekeeping are inhibited,[3] In addition corruption, and criminal exploitation are exacerbated.[4] Social distancing may increase feelings of isolation and alienation in ways potentially conducive to radicalization.[5] Refugees and displaced persons,[6] as well as persons living in poverty and slums, are particularly vulnerable.[7] Fragile societies are especially vulnerable to COVID-19 and conflict.[8] Lack of government capacity—or will—to address the pandemic's effects in fragile communities has led communities and criminal enterprises (OCGs and CAGs) to exploit the situation for profit and power.[9]

COVID-19 Situation Report

While the full effects of the COVID-19 pandemic are still ahead of us, some early impressions about the outbreak's effects on governance and security are possible. This work seeks to outline the contours of the situation—in effect serving as a situation report (SITREP) on COVID-19, gangs, and conflict. After introductory material—the prologue "COVID-19, Gangs, Statemaking, Threats, and Opportunities" by Steven Dudley of *InSight Crime* and the foreword "Pandemics and Conflict" by Nils Gilman, of the Berggruen Institute—followed by this introduction, the text is divided into three parts.

Part 1: Strategic Notes contains six chapters comprised of strategic notes from the Small Wars Journal-El Centro series on third generation gangs and Mexican cartels. Chapter 1 by John P. Sullivan, José de Arimatéia da Cruz and Robert J. Bunker looks at the imposition of curfews by gangs in Rio de Janeiro. In Chapter 2, Juan Ricardo Gómez Hecht joins Sullivan and Bunker to look at the quarantine and stay at home orders imposed by *maras* in El Salvador. Chapter 3 is an assessment of cartel humanitarian response activities in Mexico by Bunker and Sullivan, while Chapter 4 by Sullivan and Bunker looks at gangs and lockdown in Cape Town. In Chapter 5, Alexandra Phelan is joined by Sullivan and Bunker in looking at how revolutionaries and criminal bands (BACRIM) are exploiting COVID-19 in Colombia. Chapter 7 closes the first section with an exploration of COVID-19 and transnational Italian mafias by Anna Sergi, joined by Sullivan and Bunker.

Part 2: Essays contains seven chapters. The first, Chapter 8, by Colonel (retired) Joseph J. Collins, assesses future US national security concerns rising from the COVID-19 crisis. Vanda Felbab-Brown and Paul Wise look at pandemics and slums in Chapter 8, while Paul R. Kan looks at the pandemic's potentials for crime and conflict in Chapter 9. Keith Mines and Steven Hege consider potential opportunities enabled by the pandemic in Venezuela in Chapter 10. Nancy Lindborg discusses the need for resilience in the face of the coronavirus in fragile states in Chapter 11. Chapter 12, by Jonathan Lancelot, looks at the potential national security lessons learned from COVID-19 for cyber-defense against future 'cyber-states.' The section closes with a discussion of potential mechanisms to address hybrid threats involving future bioweapons.[10]

Part 3: Potentials contains a conclusion by Bunker and Sullivan followed by an afterword, postscript, appendix, and selected readings. The afterword "Terrorism, Biosecurity, and COVID-19," by Colin P. Clarke explores the prospects for future biological terrorism involving infectious diseases. The postscript, by Tuesday Reitano, returns the text to a discussion of pandemics and transnational organized crime. The appendix summarizes the findings of a pandemic war game, 'Urban Outbreak 2019,' emphasizing civil-military response that was conducted at the US Naval War College. The results and lessons learned from the game's after-action review (AAR) findings can inform future preparedness efforts.

Conclusion

The COVID-19 pandemic is influencing future governance—both traditional and criminal—and, as such, exemplifies the process of state-making and state transition.[11] The pandemic also appears to be expanding the power and reach of organized crime (OCGs), including mafias, gangs, and militias (CAGs) through the combination of an absence of effective state action (presence and capacity) which expand the capacity of these challengers to the state and utilitarian provision of humanitarian goods to communities ravaged by the pandemic.[12] Of course, humanitarian action and criminal governance does not remove the potential for predatory action by these groups. It does, however, contribute to a change in the nature of governance, security, and the relationship between these OCGs, the state, illicit markets, and the communities they operate within. This collection seeks to examine these unfolding dynamics and future potentials.

Endnotes

[1] See "America's far right is energised by covid-19 lockdowns." *The Economist*. 17 May 2020, https://www.economist.com/united-states/2020/05/17/americas-far-right-is-energised-by-covid-19-lockdowns;

Masood Farivar, "How Far-Right Extremists Are Exploiting the COVID Pandemic." *Voice of America*. 25 April 2020, https://www.voanews.com/covid-19-pandemic/how-far-right-extremists-are-exploiting-covid-pandemic; Luke Baker, "Militants, fringe groups exploiting COVID-19, warns EU anti-terrorism chief." Reuters. 30 April 2020, https://www.reuters.com/article/us-health-coronavirus-eu-security/militants-fringe-groups-exploiting-covid-19-warns-eu-anti-terrorism-chief-idUSKBN22C2HG; and Miranda Christou, "COVID-19 has exposed the odd conspiracy links between left and right." *openDemocracy*. 13 May 2020, https://www.opendemocracy.net/en/countering-radical-right/covid-19-has-exposed-odd-conspiracy-links-between-left-and-right/.

[2] While the notion that public health measures curtail liberty has a long history, courts at all levels, including the US Supreme Court, have long held that the Constitution allows the imposition of reasonable nonconsensual and coercive measures to control an epidemic. In this context, the scope of "reasonable" action is determined by public heath officials. See Adam Klein and Benjamin Wittes, "The Long History of Coercive Health Responses in American Law." *Lawfare*. 13 April 2020, https://www.lawfareblog.com/long-history-coercive-health-responses-american-law and Robert Chesney, "The Quarantine Power: A Primer in Light of the Coronavirus Situation." *Lawfare*. 7 February 2020, https://www.lawfareblog.com/quarantine-power-primer-light-coronavirus-situation.

[3] "The Covid-19 Pandemic and Deadly Conflict." International Crisis Group. N.D., https://www.crisisgroup.org/pandemics_public_health_deadly_conflict.

[4] "Fighting corruption during the coronavirus." *Global Initiative Against Transnational Organized Crime*. 3 June 2020, https://globalinitiative.net/corruption-coronavirus/ and Paul R. Kan, "Special Commentary: Outbreak: COVID-19, Crime, and Conflict." *Special Commentary: COVID-19* (Strategic Studies institute), 14 May 2020, https://ssi.armywarcollege.edu/wp-content/uploads/2020/05/COVID-19-Crime-and-Conflict_Kan_v1.1_post.pdf.

[5] See William Avis, "The COVID-19 pandemic and response on violent extremist recruitment and radicalization." *K4D Helpdesk*. 4 May 2020, https://reliefweb.int/sites/reliefweb.int/files/resources/808_COVID19%20_and_Violent_Extremism.pdf and Eric Rosand, Khalid Koser, and Lilla Schumicky-Logan, "Preventing violent extremism during and after the COVID-19 pandemic." Brookings. 28 April 2002, https://www.brookings.edu/blog/order-from-chaos/2020/04/28/preventing-violent-extremism-during-and-after-the-covid-19-pandemic/.

[6] Samuel Volkin, "How Are Refugees Affected By Covid-19 (Interview of Paul Spiegel)." *HUB*. 20 April 2020, https://hub.jhu.edu/2020/04/20/covid-19-refugees-asylum-seekers/.

[7] Vanda Felbab-Brown and Paul H. Wise, "When pandemics come to slums." Brookings. 6 April 2020, https://www.brookings.edu/blog/order-from-chaos/2020/04/06/when-pandemics-come-to-slums/.

[8] Corinne Graff, "COVID-19 and Conflict: Implications for Fragile Societies." *The Olive Branch* (United States Institute of Peace Blog). 4 June 2020, https://www.usip.org/index.php/blog/2020/06/covid-19-and-conflict-implications-fragile-societies.

[9] Ines Eisele, "Brazil's favelas forced to fight coronavirus alone." DW (Deutsche Welle). 2 July 2020, https://www.dw.com/en/brazils-favelas-forced-to-fight-coronavirus-alone/a-54031886?maca=en-Twitter-sharing.

[10] An excellent discussion of future terrorist threat potentials, including biological terrorism, is seen in Paul Cruickshank and Don Rassler, "A View from the CT Foxhole: A Virtual Roundtable on COVID-19 and Counterterrorism with Audrey Kurth Cronin, Lieutenant General (Ret) Michael Nagata, Magnus Ranstorp, Ali Soufan, and Juan Zarate." *CTC Sentinel*, Special Issue on COVID-19 & Counterterrorism. Vol. 13, Issue 6, June 2020, https://ctc.usma.edu/a-view-from-the-ct-foxhole-a-virtual-roundtable-on-covid-19-and-counterterrorism-with-audrey-kurth-cronin-lieutenant-general-ret-michael-nagata-magnus-ranstorp-ali-soufan-and-juan-zarate/.

[11] See Nicholas Barnes and Julian Albarracín, "Criminal Governance in the Time of COVID-19." Word on the Street (Urban Violence Research Network). 6 July 2020, https://urbanviolence.org/criminal-governance-in-the-time-of-covid-19/; "COVID 19 and organized crime: »Latin American governments are in a state-making competition with crime« (Interview with Vanda Felbab-Brown and Ariel Ávila)." Friedrich-Ebert-Stiftung. 12 May 2020, https://www.fes.de/e/when-will-latin-american-governments-realize-that-they-are-in-a-state-building-competition-with-organized-crime-did-covid-19-change-the-game; John P. Sullivan, "How Illicit Networks Impact Sovereignty," Chapter 10. Michael Miklaucic and Jacqueline Brewer, Eds. *Convergence: Illicit Networks and National Security in the Age of Globalization*. Washington, DC: National Defense University Press, 2015: pp. 171-187; and of course, Charles Tilly, "War Making and State Making as Organized Crime." Peter B. Evans, Dietrich Rueschemeyer, and Theda Skopol, Eds. *Bringing the State Back In*, Cambridge: Cambridge University Press, 1985: pp. 169-191.

[12] On power acquisition, see Ryan Berg and Andrea Varsori, "COVID-19 is increasing the power of Brazil's criminal groups." *LSE Latin America and Caribbean Blog*. 28 May 2020, https://blogs.lse.ac.uk/

latamcaribbean/2020/05/28/covid-19-is-increasing-the-power-of-brazils-criminal-groups/. On provision of humanitarian aid by OCGs see, John P. Sullivan, "Criminal Insurgency: Narcocultura, Social Banditry, and Information Operations." *Small Wars Journal*. 3 December 2012, https://smallwarsjournal.com/jrnl/art/criminal-insurgency-narcocultura-social-banditry-and-information-operations.

Part 1

Strategic Notes

Chapter 1

Third Generation Gangs Strategic Note No. 22: Rio's Gangs Impose Curfews in Response to Coronavirus

John P. Sullivan, José de Arimatéia da Cruz and Robert J. Bunker

First Published in Small Wars Journal on 10 April 2020

In response to the COVID-19 pandemic and fears of the spread of the coronavirus through Rio de Janeiro's densely populated *favelas* local gangs (*gangues*) and militias (*milícias*) are imposing social controls in the form of curfews to limit the spread of the disease. The Red Command (*Comando Vermelho*) gang is specifically mentioned in this context with numerous reports discussing their imposition of a coronavirus curfew in the *Cidade de Deus* (City of God) *favela* while the role of other gangs and militias is suggested in the reportage.

Cidade de Deus (City of God) Favela, Rio de Janeiro, Brazil (Public Domain) Photographer Junius, Wikimedia Commons, https://commons.wikimedia.org/wiki/File:Cidade_de_Deus.jpg.

Key Information: Andres Schipani and Bryan Harris, "Drug gangs in Brazil's favelas enforce coronavirus lockdown." *Financial Times*. 26 March 2020, https://www.ft.com/content/aaef1591-2fc5-4e6f-ab84-0e83b5a146ca?segmentId=114a04fe-353d-37db-f705-204c9a0a157b:

> The messages first arrived via WhatsApp. Stay home or else.
>
> It was a stark warning to the residents of Brazil's densely populated slums — but not one delivered by federal government, health officials or even state police.
>
> With president Jair Bolsonaro dismissing the pandemic as "sniffles" and criticising regional lockdown measures, the country's drug gangs and paramilitary groups have stepped in to enforce social distancing to combat the spread of coronavirus.

Key Information: Caio Barretto Briso and Tom Phillips, "Brazil gangs impose strict curfews to slow coronavirus spread." *The Guardian*. 25 March 2020, https://www.theguardian.com/world/2020/mar/25/brazil-rio-gangs-coronavirus:

> Drug traffickers in one of Rio de Janeiro's best-known favelas have imposed a coronavirus curfew, amid growing fears over the impact the virus could have on some of Brazil's poorest citizens…
>
> In recent days, as Brazil's coronavirus death toll has climbed to 46 gang members have been circulating in the Cidade de Deus (City of God) favela in western Rio ordering residents to remain indoors after 8pm…
>
> …in an apparent attempt to prevent further infections the Red Command gang leaders who control the favela have ordered residents to stay at home.
>
> A video apparently recorded in the City of God circulated on social media this week showing a loudspeaker broadcasting the alert: "Anyone found messing or walking around outside will be punished."

Key Information: "Coronavírus: traficantes e milicianos impõem toque de recolher em comunidades do Rio." *G1, O Globo.* 23 March 2020, https://g1.globo.com/rj/rio-de-janeiro/noticia/2020/03/23/coronavirus-traficantes-e-milicianos-impoem-toque-de-recolher-em-comunidades-do-rio.ghtml:

> Indo além das medidas tomas pelo estado, recado enviado pelas redes sociais nas comunidades de Rio das Pedras, Muzema e Tijuquinha, na Zona Oeste do Rio, orienta que a população não saia das ruas a partir das 20h.
>
> **"Atenção todos os moradores de Rio das Pedras, Muzema e Tijuquinha!!! Toque de recolher a partir de hoje 20:00 hrs. Quem for visto na rua após este horário vai aprender a respeitar o próximo!!!".**
>
> Já em outra publicação, a nota ordena o toque de recolher todos os dias, no mesmo horário, e diz:
>
> **"Queremos o melhor para população. Se o governo não tem capacidade de dar um jeito, o crime organizado resolve".**[1]

Key Information: Agência O Globo, "Coronavírus: tráfico e milícia ordenam toque de recolher em favelas do Rio." *Úlitimo Segundo.* 24 March 2020, https://ultimosegundo.ig.com.br/brasil/2020-03-24/coronavirus-trafico-e-milicia-ordenam-toque-de-recolher-em-favelas-do-rio.html:

> **Traficantes** e **milicianos** estabeleceram toques de recolher em favelas após a confirmação de casos de infecções de **coronavírus** em comunidades do **Rio de Janeiro**. Os criminosos também fazem ameaças a moradores que forem flagrados circulando pelas **favelas** após às 20h. Na **Cidade de Deus**, na Zona Oeste, primeira comunidade do Rio a ter um caso confirmado, os traficantes circularam pela favela com um alto-falante durante a tarde de ontem.[2]

Key Information: Ricardo Moraes, Debora Moreira, and Rodrigo Viga Gaier, "Gangs call curfews as coronavirus hits Rio favelas." Reuters. 24 March 2020, https://www.reuters.com/article/us-health-coronavirus-brazil-favelas-fea/gangs-call-curfews-as-coronavirus-hits-rio-favelas-idUSKBN21B3EV:

City of God, a sprawling complex of slums made famous in a hit 2002 movie of the same name, registered the first confirmed case of coronavirus in Rio's favelas over the weekend.

Now, with the state government woefully underfunded and Brazilian President Jair Bolsonaro widely criticized for a slow response to the outbreak, criminal gangs that have long held sway across Rio's favelas are taking their own precautions against the virus, according to residents and press reports.

According to well-sourced Rio newspaper Extra, City of God gangsters have been driving round the slum, blaring out a recorded message to residents.

"We're imposing a curfew because nobody is taking this seriously," the message said, according to Extra's Tuesday story. "Whoever is in the street screwing around or going for a walk will receive a corrective and serve as an example. Better to stay home doing nothing. The message has been given."

Third Generation Gang Analysis

The social impact of the coronavirus and COVID-19 pandemic is challenging both states and criminal enterprises worldwide.[3] The imposition of curfews and social controls by territorial gangs poses unique challenges to governance and pandemic response.[4] This type of alternate governance also poses challenges to state solvency as the gangs and militias (criminal armed groups or CAGs) compete with the state for legitimacy and the provision of social goods. This provision of 'utilitarian social goods' can contribute limited public health and safety but can also be used by the imposing CAGs to alter the allocation of power among the state and criminal rivals to their advantage.[5] The competition between state and criminal enterprises (including criminal insurgents) is a facet of state transition as discussed by Tilly, Sullivan, Bunker, and Kilcullen.[6]

The gangs—in this case Rio's *Comando Vermhelo*—are acting in the manner of social bandits as describes by Hobsbawn and later by Sullivan in the context of criminal insurgents.[7] That is the gangs seek relative power and legitimacy in order to secure enterprises community support and freedom of movement. Previous CAGs (criminal cartels) providing humanitarian aid have been documented in Mexico.[8] More recently, the Gulf Cartel and Los Viagras have been reported to be providing humanitarian food distribution to communities challenged by the pandemic.[9] In El Salvador gangs are also regulating social movement—including enforced social distancing—to limit the spread of the coronavirus and exert territorial control.[10]

The Red Command (*Comando Vermelho*) flyer originally appearing on WhatsApp. [Gang Social Media]. Reposted by TROPA DO CV @proibidoparar, 22 March 2020, https://twitter.com/proibidoparar/status/1241868747637391362/photo/1.

The COVID-19 outbreak poses many challenges in the favelas (and other urban settings). As Robert Muggah recently told *The New Humanitarian*, "In some cases, aid agencies are also required to work with, or alongside, non-state providers, including armed groups. For example, in some Brazilian, Colombian, and Mexican cities organised crime and self-defence groups are engaged in social service provision, raising complex questions for aid providers about whether and how to support vulnerable communities."[11]

These vulnerable populations—living in slums and *favelas*—are often deprived basic lifelines like adequate potable water supply, sewage, and public services like policing. The gangs and CAGs often fill the void in governance and in collusion with corrupt public officials provide access to services.[12] This demands public accountability and engaging in humanitarian negotiations and diplomacy by aid providers with the CAGs (gangs, cartels, and militias).[13] Brazilian public health authorities seeing the gravity of the situation are initiating humanitarian negotiations with organized crime leaders:

> O governo federal prepara uma estratégia de combate ao novo coronavírus nas favelas brasileiras que buscará amparo de lideranças ligadas ao crime organizado. Segundo o ministro da Saúde, Luiz Henrique Mandetta, a pasta está disposta a dialogar com chefes do tráfico e de milícias para conseguir apoio às medidas de isolamento.
>
> "A saúde dialoga, sim, com o tráfico, com a milícia, porque também são seres humanos e precisam colaborar, ajudar, participar. Então, neste momento, quando a gente faz esse tipo de colocação, a gente deixa claro que todo mundo vai colaborar (no combate à covid-19)", disse o ministro durante coletiva de imprensa nesta quarta-feira, 8 [April] [14][15]

The interaction between CAGs—criminal cartels, gangs, militias, and mafias—is complex and historically has varied by time and place. Crises like global pandemics can potentially change these dynamics as seen in the case of COVID-18 in Brazil's *favelas* (and elsewhere). Terrorists, rebels, and insurgents (both political and criminal) are likely to exploit the pandemic to further their goals.[16] States are also likely to seek to build upon humanitarian initiatives as a means of stabilizing communities and reducing criminal violence. The success of these efforts—for all participants—remains to be seen. As the pandemic matures, these interactions are likely to provide new data points and case studies for evaluation.

Sources

Agência O Globo, "Coronavírus: tráfico e milícia ordenam toque de recolher em favelas do Rio." *Úlitimo Segundo*. 24 March 2020, https://ultimosegundo.ig.com.br/brasil/2020-03-24/coronavirus-trafico-e-milicia-ordenam-toque-de-recolher-em-favelas-do-rio.html.

Parker Asmann. "What Does Coronavirus Mean for Criminal Governance in Latin America?" *InSight Crime*. 31 March 2020, https://www.insightcrime.org/news/analysis/criminal-governance-latin-america-coronavirus/.

Caio Barretto Briso and Tom Phillips, "Brazil gangs impose strict curfews to slow coronavirus spread." *The Guardian*. 25 March 2020, https://www.theguardian.com/world/2020/mar/25/brazil-rio-gangs-coronavirus.

"Coronavírus: traficantes e milicianos impõem toque de recolher em comunidades do Rio." *G1, O Globo*. 23 March 2020, https://g1.globo.com/rj/rio-de-janeiro/noticia/2020/03/23/coronavirus-traficantes-e-milicianos-impoem-toque-de-recolher-em-comunidades-do-rio.ghtml.

Steven Eisenhammer, "Mistrustful of state, Brazil slum hires own doctors to fight virus." Reuters. 2 April 2020, https://www.reuters.com/article/us-health-coronavirus-brazil-favela-feat/mistrustful-of-state-brazil-slum-hires-own-doctors-to-fight-virus-idUSKBN21L08Y?il=0.

Vanda Felbab-Brown, "How COVID-19 is changing law enforcement practices by police and criminal groups." *Brookings*. 7 April 2020, https://www.brookings.edu/blog/order-from-chaos/2020/04/07/how-covid-19-is-changing-law-enforcement-practices-by-police-and-by-criminal-groups/.

Vanda Felbab-Brown and Paul Wise, "When pandemics come to slums." *Brookings*. 6 April 2020, https://www.brookings.edu/blog/order-from-chaos/2020/04/06/when-pandemics-come-to-slums/.

Ricardo Moraes, Debora Moreira, and Rodrigo Viga Gaier, "Gangs call curfews as coronavirus hits Rio favelas." Reuters. 24 March 2020, https://www.reuters.com/article/us-health-coronavirus-brazil-favelas-fea/gangs-call-curfews-as-coronavirus-hits-rio-favelas-idUSKBN21B3EV.

Andres Schipani and Bryan Harris, "Drug gangs in Brazil's favelas enforce coronavirus lockdown." *Financial Times*. 26 March 2020, https://www.ft.com/content/aaef1591-2fc5-4e6f-ab84-0e83b5a146ca?segmentId=114a04fe-353d-37db-f705-204c9a0a157b.

Endnotes

[1] In English the excerpted text reads: "Going beyond the measures taken by the state, a message sent by social networks in the communities of Rio das Pedras, Muzema and Tijuquinha, in the West Zone of Rio, advises that the population does not leave the streets after 8 pm. 'Attention all residents of Rio das Pedras, Muzema and Tijuquinha !!! …Curfew starting today 20:00 hrs. Whoever is seen on the street after this time will learn to respect the next one !!!'." In another publication, the note orders the curfew every day, at the

same time, and says: "We want the best for the population. If the government does not have the capacity to fix it, organized crime will solve it."

[2] In English the excerpted text reads: "Traffickers and militiamen established curfews in *favelas* after confirmation of cases of coronavirus infections in communities in Rio de Janeiro. Criminals also make threats to residents who are caught circulating in the *favelas* after 8 pm. In Cidade de Deus, in the West Zone, the first community in Rio to have a confirmed case, the traffickers circulated through the *favela* with a loudspeaker yesterday afternoon."

[3] See for example, Parker Asmann. "What Does Coronavirus Mean for Criminal Governance in Latin America?" *InSight Crime*. 31 March 2020, https://www.insightcrime.org/news/analysis/criminal-governance-latin-america-coronavirus/, Richard Behar, "Organized Crime In The Time of Corona. *Forbes*. 27 March 2020, https://www.forbes.com/sites/richardbehar/2020/03/27/organized-crime-in-the-time-of-corona/#53c25c4f150, and "Crime and Contagion: The impact of a pandemic on organized Crime." *Policy Brief*. Global Initiative Against Transnational Crime. March 2020, https://globalinitiative.net/crime-contagion-impact-covid-crime/.

[4] See John P. Sullivan, "The Challenges of Territorial Gangs: Civil Strife, Criminal Insurgencies and Crime Wars." *Revista do Ministério Público Militar* (Brazil), Ediçãon. 31, November 2019, https://www.academia.edu/40917684/The_Challenges_of_Territorial_Gangs_Civil_Strife_Criminal_Insurgencies_and_Crime_Wars and Vanda Felbab-Brown and Paul Wise, "When pandemics come to slums." *Brookings*. 6 April 2020, https://www.brookings.edu/blog/order-from-chaos/2020/04/06/when-pandemics-come-to-slums/.

[5] The potential for criminal advantage via the utilitarian provision of social goods is discussed by Felbab-Brown and Paul Wise, Ibid, note 4.

[6] See Charles Tilly, War Making and State Making as Organized Crime" in *Bringing the State Back In*. Peter B. Evans, Dietrich Rueschemeyer and Theda Skocpol, Eds. Cambridge: Cambridge University Press, 1985: pp. 169–91; John P. Sullivan, "How Illicit Networks Impact Sovereignty": Chapter 10 in Michael Miklaucic and Jacqueline Brewer, Eds. *Convergence: Illicit Networks in the Age of Globalization*. Washington, DC: National Defense University Press, 2013: pp. 171-188; John P. Sullivan and Robert J. Bunker, "Rethinking insurgency: criminality, spirituality, and societal warfare in the Americas," *Small Wars & Insurgencies*. Vol. 22, Issue 5, 2011: pp. 742-763, https://www.tandfonline.com/action/

showCitFormats?doi=10.1080%2F09592318.2011.625720 and David Kilcullen, *Out of the Mountains—The Coming Age of the Urban Guerilla*, New York: Oxford University Press, 2013, p. 126.

[7] See Eric Hobsbawm, *Bandits*. New York: The New Press, 2000, 1969 and John P. Sullivan, "Criminal Insurgency: Narcocultura, Social Banditry, and Information Operations." *Small Wars Journal*. 3 December 2012, https://smallwarsjournal.com/jrnl/art/criminal-insurgency-narcocultura-social-banditry-and-information-operations.

[8] John P. Sullivan, "Mexican Cartel Strategic Note No. 15: Skullduggery or Social Banditry? Cartel Humanitarian Aid." *Small Wars Journal*. 25 November 2013, https://smallwarsjournal.com/blog/mexican-cartel-strategic-note-no-15-skullduggery-or-social-banditry-cartel-humanitarian-aid and John P. Sullivan and Robert J. Bunker, "Mexican Cartel Strategic Note No. 24: Cartel and Gang Provision of Post-Earthquake Humanitarian Aid." *Small Wars Journal*. 21 October 2017, https://smallwarsjournal.com/jrnl/art/mexican-cartel-strategic-note-no-24-cartel-and-gang-provision-post-earthquake-humanitarian.

[9] Laura Mallene, "Mexican Drug Cartel Gives Out Food to the Poor Amid Pandemic." *OCCRP: Organized Crime and Corruption Reporting Project*. 7 April 2020, https://www.occrp.org/en/daily/12038-mexican-drug-cartel-gives-out-food-to-the-poor-amid-pandemic and "Integrantes De El Cartel Del Golfo Entrega Despensas Por Covid-19 En Tamaulipas." *Blog del Narco*. 4 April 2020, https://elblogdelnarco.com/2020/04/05/integrantes-de-el-cartel-del-golfo-entrega-despensas-por-covid-19-en-tamaulipas/.

[10] Kate Linthicum. Molly O'Toole, and Alexander Renderos, "In El Salvador, gangs are enforcing the coronavirus lockdown with baseball bats." *Los Angeles Times*. 7 April 2020, https://www.latimes.com/world-nation/story/2020-04-07/el-salvador-coronavirus-homicides-bukele.

[11] Robert Muggah quoted in Andrew Gully, "Coronavirus in the city: A Q&A on the catastrophe confronting the urban poor." *The New Humanitarian*. 1 April 2020, https://www.thenewhumanitarian.org/interview/2020/04/01/coronavirus-cities-urban-poor?utm_source=twitter&utm_medium=social&utm_campaign=social.

[12] Vanda Felbab-Brown and Paul Wise, "When pandemics come to slums." *Brookings*. 6 April 2020, notes 3 & 4.

[13] See for example, Hugo van den Eertwegh, "Negotiating with Criminal Groups: From Prejudice to Pragmatism." Geneva Peacebuilding Platform, *Paper No. 18*. 2016, https://www.gpplatform.ch/sites/

default/files/PP18%20Negotiating%20with%20Criminal%20Groups%20-%20From%20Prejudice%20to%20Pragmatism_0.pdf.

[14] Julia Lindner and André Borges, "Ministério dialoga com o tráfico e a milícia, diz Mandetta." *Terra*. 8 April 2020, https://www.terra.com.br/vida-e-estilo/saude/ministerio-dialoga-com-o-trafico-e-a-milicia-diz-mandetta,90e4627d550049272f8242e7b94c75e9qwxjeix4.html. In English the excerpted text reads: "'The federal government is preparing a strategy to combat the new coronavirus in Brazilian favelas that will seek support from leaders linked to organized crime. According to the Minister of Health, Luiz Henrique Mandetta, the portfolio is willing to dialogue with drug and militia leaders to obtain support for the isolation measures… Health dialogues, yes, with the traffic, with the militia, because they are also human beings and they need to collaborate, help, participate. So, at this moment, when we do this type of placement, we make it clear that everyone will collaborate (in combating the covid-19)', said the minister during a press conference this Wednesday, 8 [April]."

[15] Also see, "Ministério da Saúde está disposto a dialogar com o tráfico e com a milícia, diz Mandetta." *O Popular*. 8 April 2020, https://www.opopular.com.br/noticias/cidades/minist%C3%A9rio-da-sa%C3%BAde-est%C3%A1-disposto-a-dialogar-com-o-tr%C3%A1fico-e-com-a-mil%C3%ADcia-diz-mandetta-1.2032049.

[16] Colin P. Clarke, "Yesterday's Terrorists Are Today's Public-Health Providers." *Foreign Policy*. 8 April 2020, https://foreignpolicy.com/2020/04/08/terrorists-nonstate-ungoverned-health-providers-coronavirus-pandemic/.

For Additional Reading

"Crime and Contagion: The impact of a pandemic on organized Crime." *Policy Brief.* Global Initiative Against Transnational Crime. March 2020.

Vanda Felbab-Brown, "How COVID-19 is changing law enforcement practices by police and criminal groups." *Brookings*, 7 April 2020.

John P. Sullivan and Robert J. Bunker, Eds. *Strategic Notes on Third Generation Gangs*. A Small Wars Journal-El Centro Anthology. Bloomington: Xlibris, 2020.

John P. Sullivan, "The Challenges of Territorial Gangs: Civil Strife, Criminal Insurgencies and Crime Wars." *Revista do Ministério Público Militar* (Brazil), Edição n. 31, November 2019.

Chapter 2

Third Generation Gangs Strategic Note No. 23: El Salvadoran Gangs (Maras) Enforce Domestic Quarantine / Stay at Home Orders (Cuarentena domiciliar)

John P. Sullivan, Robert J. Bunker and Juan Ricardo Gómez Hecht

First Published in Small Wars Journal on 5 May 2020

Salvadoran *maras* (gangs) have adapted to the COVID-19 outbreak by enforcing social control in the form of domestic quarantine (*cuarentena domiciliar),* curfews, and social distancing. The major *maras*, i.e. MS-13, and the *Sureños* and *Revolucionarios* factions of Barrio 18 (Eighteenth Street), have communicated this 'public health' dictate throughout the territories they control. In addition to enforcing domestic 'quarantine,' the Barrio 18 factions have suspended collecting 'street taxes' (extortion payments) while MS-13 continues to collect '*renta*' (rent).

Key Information: Kevin Sieff, Susannah George, and Kareem Fahim, "Now joining the fight against coronavirus: The world's armed rebels, drug cartels and gangs." *Washington Post*. 14 April 2020, https://www.washingtonpost.com/world/the_americas/coronavirus-taliban-ms-13-drug-cartels-gangs/2020/04/13/83aa07ac-79c2-11ea-a311-adb1344719a9_story.html:

> Last month, as the Salvadoran government was enforcing one of Latin America's earliest and most stringent lockdowns, leaders of MS-13 decided that they would institute their own curfew. It was a rare overlap of policy between the gang and the government, which have fought each other for years.

But it also reflected a reality in much of El Salvador: The police have limited access in neighborhoods under criminal control, and in those places, only a gang-enforced curfew would be observed.

Key Information: Kate Linthicum, Molly O'Toole, and Alexander Renderos, "In El Salvador, gangs are enforcing the coronavirus lockdown with baseball bats." *Los Angeles Times.* 7 April 2020, https://www.latimes.com/world-nation/story/2020-04-07/el-salvador-coronavirus-homicides-bukele:

> The street gangs that have long terrorized El Salvador have now turned their attention from extortion and killing to a more pressing matter: enforcing social distancing restrictions, often with threats and baseball bats…
>
> In many parts of the country, the gangs are more effective than government authorities, with tactics that include circulating recordings on messaging applications threatening people who break the rules…
>
> The gangs have also produced videos showing masked members hitting people for not adhering to the quarantine.

Key Information: Carlos Martínez, Óscar Martínez, and Efren Lemus, "Pandillas amenazan a quien incumpla la cuarentena." *El Faro.* 18 April 2020, https://elfaro.net/es/202003/el_salvador/24211/Pandillas-amenazan-a-quien-incumpla-la-cuarentena.htm:

> Representantes de las tres pandillas confirmaron a El Faro que este 30 de marzo decidieron amenazar a los habitantes que incumplan la cuarentena nacional. La extorsión impuesta por las pandillas también ha sido modificada por la crisis del coronavirus. En zonas concretas, dicen, han perdonado el cobro criminal a algunos vendedores informales. El otras zonas, simplemente no han podido recogerlo debido a la presencia masiva de fuerzas del Estado en las calles.
>
> El Faro habló con líderes nacionales de la MS-13, de la facción Sureños del Barrio 18 y dos pandilleros de la facción Revolucionarios, así como con transportistas, vendedores informales y un comisionado policial y obtuvo mensajes de voz enviados por las diferentes

pandillas a sus estructuras en los territorios que controlan. En esos mensajes, las pandillas amenazan a cualquier vecino que circule en la calle por una razón distinta a ir a comprar alimentos a "vérselas directamente con nosotros".[1]

Key Information: "Matones de la salud: En El Salvador, las pandillas dejaron de matarse y ahora vigilan el cumplimiento de la cuarentena." *Clarín Internacional*. 9 April 2020, https://www.clarin.com/internacional/salvador-pandillas-dejaron-matarse-ahora-vigilan-cumplimiento-cuarentena_0_gmonzeZOr.html:

> Lo que impulsa el declive no es una tregua entre pandillas o una nueva estrategia policial, sino una cuarentena nacional de semanas para frenar la propagación del coronavirus.
>
> Las pandillas callejeras que durante mucho tiempo han aterrorizado a El Salvador, ahora desviaron su atención de la extorsión y los asesinatos a un asunto más apremiante: imponer restricciones de distanciamiento social, a menudo mediante amenazas y violencia.[2]

Key Information: Marcos Alemán (AP), "El Salvador combate el coronavirus y se reduce la violencia." *San Diego Union-Tribune en Español*. 1 April 2020, https://www.sandiegouniontribune.com/en-espanol/noticias/story/2020-04-01/el-salvador-combate-el-coronavirus-y-se-reduce-la-violencia:

> Desde el martes circularon audios de supuestos pandilleros de la Mara Salvatrucha en los que amenazan con represalias a las personas que no acaten las órdenes del gobierno de mantenerse en cuarentena familiar.
>
> Luego aparecieron dos videos en los que se observa cuando supuestos pandilleros a los que no se les ve los rostros, armados con bates de beisbol, golpean en las piernas y los glúteos a personas que al parecer no han acatado la orden de no salir de sus casas.[3]

Key Information: "Circulan supuestos audios de pandilleros que piden acatar la cuarentena." *elsalvador.com*. 31 March 2020, https://www.elsalvador.com/noticias/coronavirus-pandillas-ms-amenaza-cuarentena/701446/2020/:

En un audio que circulan en redes, dicen que implantan sus propias reglas para castigar a quienes irrespeten la cuarentena impuesta por el Gobierno. Si ven a alguien sin mascarilla le llamarán la atención. Si desobedece, "tomarán otras medidas".

Desde el lunes al final de la tarde, diversos audios o mensajes de texto comenzaron a circular en cadenas de WhatsApp, en las que, presuntamente, pandilleros advierten que como **al Gobierno se le ha salido de control las medidas para contener el COVID-19, ellos** vigilarán que tales medidas sean cumplidas en los territorios donde ellos tienen pleno dominio territorial.[4]

Third Generation Gang Analysis

The COVID-19 outbreak has profound national and biosecurity implications. In addition to significant health consequences (morbidity and mortality) and social control implications regarding quarantine and social distancing, the coronavirus pandemic has altered the human terrain and operating space for organized crime, mafias, and gangs. In the preceding Third Generation Gangs Strategic Note (No. 22), Sullivan, Arimatéia da Cruz, and Bunker examined the COVID-19 curfew situation in Rio's *favelas*.[5] In this note, the analysis is expanded to look at the situation in El Salvador. *Maras* are a significant force in El Salvador's criminal and political landscape.[6] These *maras* (sophisticated, third generation gangs) dominate local *pandillas* (smaller, less-sophisticated gangs) and challenge the state monopoly on force and political power. The largest *maras* are Mara Salvatrucha (known as MS-13) and Barrio 18 (Eighteenth Street). Both are transnational in nature and alter the nature of sovereignty and governance in a process of criminal insurgency.[7]

Maras like MS-13 are active in about 94% of El Salvador's municipalities, forming 'other governed spaces' or 'criminal enclaves' known as '*zonas rojas*' (red zones) where the gangs exert *de facto* territorial and social control.[8] In the current global health crisis, the *maras* have become players in the provision of public health, social control, and in some cases humanitarian aid. In all of these cases, the provision of social goods is opportunistic, supporting the gangs' needs. In that sense, the active engagement of *maras*, gangs, mafias, and criminal cartels is essentially 'the utilitarian provision of social goods' and often characterized as 'social banditry.'[9]

Gang beating of a local individual (On buttocks with a bat repeatedly) for a quarantine enforcement violation. *Mara* posting on social media; Gang colors and context suggest MS-13. Note—the gang member is wearing a protective facemask. [1:13 second phone video at 0:26 second mark]. Source: "Circula vídeo de presuntos pandilleros que golpean a un hombre por salir a la calle." *elsalvador.com*. 1 April 2020, https://www.elsalvador.com/noticias/nacional/cuarentena-pandillas-amenazas-golpiza/701785/2020/.

The pandemic crisis provides a range of opportunities and threats to territorial criminal enterprises. The opportunity to provide social control in the form of humanitarian aid and advocacy, enforcing curfews, and quarantines, and suspending 'street taxes,' and *de facto* gang truces and co-operation with health initiatives can promote public perceptions of legitimacy and strengthen the gangs' power. These moves can also protect gang members from the disease itself, giving the gangs strategic advantage. This facet is also linked to enlightened self interest as the gangs recognize the need to protect themselves from the corona virus since the *mareros* fear physicians may favor non-gang members for life saving treatment like scarce ventilators.[10] In addition, these short-term factors limit immediate violence, however, when the quarantine and street tax holiday is lifted, violent competition may return.

Policía Nacional Civil (PNC) and Fuerza Armada maintain quarantine checkpoint in Puerto de la Libertad, El Salvador, 18 April 2020. Source: Secretaría de Comunicaciones de la Presidencia de la República de El Salvador, https://twitter.com/ComunicacionSV/status/1251605702071799813?s=20.

Essentially, just as criminal enterprises vary in configuration and modus operandi, so does the response of criminal enterprises to humanitarian crises and pandemics. In El Salvador, we see one example of this variation: the two largest Barrio 18 factions (*Sureños* and *Revolucionarios*) suspended collection of street taxes while MS-13 continued collecting them.[11][12][13] This variation between gangs and regions is related to the network configuration of gangs where local cliques and factions adapt to local conditions.[14] In short, as Anna Sergi has cautioned: "organised crime is not homogenous."[15]

> Poblacion salvadoreña en la presente le dejamos en claro que nos desligamos de todo mensaje que se a difundido en las redes sociales ((videos, audios, escritos)), en barrios y colonias donde controla el BARRIO 18 SUREÑOS a que se abstenga de no salir, al contrario les pedimos humildemente acaten las normas del gobierno por la emergencia que esta pasando el pais ya que su colaboracion es de suma importancia para sus hogares y nuestras familias no salgan si no es necesario de fabor les pedimoz a nuestros barrios y colonias, donde controla el BARRIO 18 SUREÑOS, nos ayuden a difundir este comunicado donde desmentimos toda amenaza a la poblacion salvadoreña al contrario estamos sintiendo el dolor del pueblo hemos decidido como BARRIO 18 ayudar en "algunas colonias del pais pero no en todas" los mas afectados y de bajos recursos.
> Por su comprencion gracias.
> ATT... BARRIO 18 SUREÑOS

Barrio 18 Sureños Communication [Mara Social Media]. Source: Reposted by @cguanacas. Twitter, 1 April 2020, https://twitter.com/cguanacas/status/1245577337871065094?s=20.[16]

Operationally the involvement of gangs (*maras*) and criminal cartels in social control, quarantine, and humanitarian aid situations poses challenges to state institutions, especially the police and military. The potential for police and military action to conflict with gang quarantine enforcement could lead to active hostilities exacerbating existing insecurity.[17] Indeed, both the police and military are new to the enforcement of such large-scale quarantine and lockdowns.[18] These challenges can also be balanced by opportunities to engage armed non-state actors (ANSAs) and criminal armed groups (CAGs) toward acceptance of humanitarian norms including the protection of health workers and facilities.[19]

Sources

Marcos Alemán (AP), "El Salvador combate el coronavirus y se reduce la violencia." *San Diego Union-Tribune en Español*. 1 April 2020, https://www.sandiegouniontribune.com/en-espanol/noticias/story/2020-04-01/el-salvador-combate-el-coronavirus-y-se-reduce-la-violencia.

"Circulan supuestos audios de pandilleros que piden acatar la cuarentena." *elsalvador.com*. 31 March 2020, https://www.elsalvador.com/noticias/coronavirus-pandillas-ms-amenaza-cuarentena/701446/2020/.

Kate Linthicum, Molly O'Toole, and Alxander Renderos, "In El Salvador, gangs are enforcing the coronavirus lockdown with baseball bats." *Los Angeles Times*. 7 April 2020, https://www.latimes.com/world-nation/story/2020-04-07/el-salvador-coronavirus-homicides-bukele.

Carlos Martínez, Óscar Martínez, and Efren Lemus, "Pandillas amenazan a quien incumpla la cuarentena." *El Faro*. 18 April 2020, https://elfaro.net/es/202003/el_salvador/24211/Pandillas-amenazan-a-quien-incumpla-la-cuarentena.htm.

"Matones de la salud: En El Salvador, las pandillas dejaron de matarse y ahora vigilan el cumplimiento de la cuarentena." *Clarín Internacional*. 9 April 2020, https://www.clarin.com/internacional/salvador-pandillas-dejaron-matarse-ahora-vigilan-cumplimiento-cuarentena_0_gmonzeZOr.html.

Miguel Patrico, "Army and Gangs Enforce Virus Curfew in El Salvador." Courthouse News Service. 8 April 2020, https://www.courthousenews.com/army-and-gangs-enforce-virus-curfew-in-el-salvador/.

Kevin Sieff, Susannah George, and Kareem Fahim, "Now joining the fight against coronavirus: The world's armed rebels, drug cartels and gangs." *Washington Post*. 14 April 2020, https://www.washingtonpost.com/world/the_americas/coronavirus-taliban-ms-13-drug-cartels-gangs/2020/04/13/83aa07ac-79c2-11ea-a311-adb1344719a9_story.html.

"La 'extraña' entrega de víveres de parte de las pandillas a las comunidades controladas por ellos." *Verdad Digital*. 11 April 2020, https://verdaddigital.com/la-extrana-entrega-de-viveres-de-parte-de-las-pandillas-a-las-comunidades-controladas-por-ellos/.

Endnotes

[1] In English, the excerpted text reads: "Representatives of the three gangs confirmed to El Faro that this March 30 they decided to threaten the inhabitants who do not comply with the national quarantine. The extortion imposed by the gangs has also been modified by the coronavirus crisis. In specific areas, they say, they have forgiven criminal charges against some informal vendors. The other areas simply have not been able to pick it up due to the massive presence of state forces on the streets…"El Faro spoke to national leaders of the MS-13, of the Sureños faction in Barrio 18 and two gang members of the Revolutionary faction, as well as transporters, informal vendors and a police commissioner, and obtained voice messages sent by the different gangs to their structures in the territories they control. In these messages, the gangs threaten any neighbor who circulates on the street for a reason other than going to buy food to 'deal directly with us'."

[2] In English, the excerpted text reads: "What drives the decline is not a gang truce or a new police strategy, but a national quarantine of weeks to curb the spread of the coronavirus … Street gangs that have long

terrorized El Salvador have now turned their attention from extortion and murder to a more pressing issue: imposing restrictions on social distancing, often through threats and violence."

[3] In English the excerpted text reads: "Since Tuesday, audios of alleged gang members of the Mara Salvatrucha have circulated in which they threaten retaliation against people who do not comply with government orders to remain in family quarantine…Then two videos appeared in which it is observed when alleged gang members who do not see their faces, armed with baseball bats, beat the legs and buttocks of people who apparently have not complied with the order not to leave their houses."

[4] In English, the excerpted text reads: "In an audio that circulates in [social] networks, they say that they implement their own rules to punish those who disrespect the quarantine imposed by the Government. If they see someone without a mask, they will catch their attention. If he disobeys, 'they will take other measures'… From Monday to late afternoon, various audios or text messages began to circulate in WhatsApp networks in which, allegedly, gang members warn that, as the Government has lost control of the measures to contain COVID-19, they will monitor that such measures are complied with in the territories where they have full territorial control'."

[5] See John P. Sullivan, José de Arimatéia da Cruz and Robert J. Bunker, "Third Generation Gangs Strategic Note No. 22: Rio's Gangs Impose Curfews in Response to Coronavirus." *Small Wars Journal*. 10 April 2020, https://smallwarsjournal.com/jrnl/art/third-generation-gangs-strategic-note-no-22-rios-gangs-impose-curfews-response-coronavirus.

[6] See "Life Under Gang Rule in El Salvador." *International Crisis Group*. 26 November 2018, https://www.crisisgroup.org/latin-america-caribbean/central-america/el-salvador/life-under-gang-rule-el-salvador.

[7] See Ximena Galvez Lima, "Inked or Not: Maras and Their Participation in El Salvador's Recent Armed Conflict." *Journal of International Humanitarian Legal Studies*. Vol. 10, Issue 2, 23 November 2019, https://doi.org/10.1163/18781527-01002002; Juan Ricardo Gómez Hecht, "Gangs in El Salvador: A New Type of Insurgency?" *Small Wars Journal*. 27 October 2017, https://smallwarsjournal.com/jrnl/art/gangs-in-el-salvador-a-new-type-of-insurgency; and John P. Sullivan, "From Drug Wars to Criminal Insurgency: Mexican Cartels, Criminal Enclaves and Criminal Insurgency in Mexico and Central America. Implications for Global Security." *Working Paper No9*. Paris: Fondation Maison des sciences de l'homme. April 2012, https://halshs.archives-ouvertes.fr/FMSH-WP/halshs-00694083.

[8] "Maras como la infame MS-13 o Mara Salvatrucha están activas en torno al 94 por ciento de los 262 municipios de El Salvador. Además de ser una constante amenaza para la seguridad pública, en muchas de las "zonas rojas" estos grupos se han convertido en la autoridad de facto del vecindario, ejerciendo un enorme control sobre la vida cotidiana de los ciudadanos que viven en los territorios con amplia presencia criminal." "Matones de la salud: En El Salvador, las pandillas dejaron de matarse y ahora vigilan el cumplimiento de la cuarentena." *Clarín Internacional*. 9 April 2020, https://www.clarin.com/internacional/salvador-pandillas-dejaron-matarse-ahora-vigilan-cumplimiento-cuarentena_0_gmonzeZOr.html.

[9] See "Third Generation Gangs Strategic Note No. 22: Rio's Gangs Impose Curfews in Response to Coronavirus," at Note 5; and John P. Sullivan, "Mexican Cartel Strategic Note No. 15: Skullduggery or Social Banditry? Cartel Humanitarian Aid." *Small Wars Journal*. 25 November 2013, https://smallwarsjournal.com/blog/mexican-cartel-strategic-note-no-15-skullduggery-or-social-banditry-cartel-humanitarian-aid.

[10] Ana María Enciso Noguera, "El coronavirus y las maras salvadoreñas: dos lados de la moneda." *Al Día*. 9 April 2020, https://aldianews.com/es/articles/politics/el-coronavirus-y-las-maras-salvadorenas-dos-lados-de-la-moneda/58138.

[11] "El estado de excepción que se decretó hace más de dos semanas en todo el país también ha trastocado su principal fuente de financiamiento: la extorsión. Las dos facciones del Barrio 18 –Sureños y Revolucionarios– han acordado dejar de exigir dinero a buena parte de los comerciantes informales que operan en sus zonas de control, mientras que la Mara Salvatrucha-13 mantiene el cobro ilegal de dinero, conocido como "renta", a pesar de que fuentes de esa pandilla reconocen que a causa de la cuarentena obligatoria y el cierre de la mayoría de comercios les está siendo muy difícil recogerlo." Carlos Martínez, Óscar Martínez, and Efren Lemus, "Pandillas amenazan a quien incumpla la cuarentena." *El Faro*. 18 April 2020, https://elfaro.net/es/202003/el_salvador/24211/Pandillas-amenazan-a-quien-incumpla-la-cuarentena.htm.

[12] As Benjamin Lessing has observed, criminal governance may aid COVID response by enforcing lockdowns and prohibiting price gouging but it can also undermine these efforts when gangs of *milícias* (militias) force bars and stores to stay open and pay monthly extortion fees. Lessing gives examples from Brazil's favelas while in this note we see similar predatory action in MS-13s refusal to suspend street taxes. See Benjamin Lessing,"#CriminalGovernance may aid #COVID response," 17 April 2020, https://twitter.com/BigBigBLessing/status/1251240300296757250?s=20; and Anita Prado and Guilherme Peixoto, "Milícia obriga reabertura de comércio da Zona Oeste e Região Metropolitana do Rio para manter cobrança

de taxas." *O Globo–G1*. 17 April 2020, https://g1.globo.com/rj/rio-de-janeiro/noticia/2020/04/17/milicia-obriga-reabertura-do-comercio-para-recolher-taxa-em-comunidades-do-rj.ghtml.

[13] See Maria Alejandra Navarrette, "Coronavirus Affects Extortion Payments in Mexico and Central America." *InSight Crime*. 13 April 2020, https://www.insightcrime.org/news/analysis/coronavirus-extortion-mexico-central-america/.

[14] See Robert J. Bunker and John P. Sullivan, "Third Generation Gangs Strategic Note No. 13: Mara Salvatrucha (MS-13) Command and Control (C2) Geographic Variations." *Small Wars Journal*. 29 January 2019, https://smallwarsjournal.com/jrnl/art/third-generation-gangs-strategic-note-no-13-mara-salvatrucha-ms-13-command-and-control-c2.

[15] See Anna Sergi, "'Organised crime' is not homogenous." 6 April 2020, https://twitter.com/SHOC_RUSI/status/1247219704671997954?s=20; and Anna Sergi, "Organised Crime and the Coronavirus-Crisis: A Research Agenda." *RUSI (Royal United Services Institute)*. 6 April 2020, https://shoc.rusi.org/coronavirusSOCresearchagenda.

[16] In English the excerpted text roughly reads: "Salvadoran people in the present we make it clear that we detach ourselves from any message that has been spread on social networks (videos, audios, writings), in *barrios* and *colonias* [neighborhoods] controlled by BARRIO 18 SUREÑOS, to refrain from not going out, on the contrary we humbly ask you to abide by the government regulations for the emergency that the country is going through since their collaboration is of utmost importance for their homes and our families do not go out if it is not necessary. We ask our *barrios* and *colonias* [neighborhoods] controlled by BARRIO 18 SUREÑOS to help us to spread this statement where we deny all threats to the Salvadoran people on the contrary we are feeling the pain of the people, we have decided as BARRIO 18 to help in 'not all but some *colonias* [neighborhoods]' those most affected and with low income. Thank you for your understanding. Sincerely... BARRIO 18 SUREÑOS."

[17] See Anna Applebaum and Briana Mawby, "Gang Violence as Armed Conflict: A New Perspective on El Salvador." *GIWPS Policy Brief*. Washington, DC: Georgetown Institute for Women Peace and Security. November 2018, https://giwps.georgetown.edu/wp-content/uploads/2018/12/Gang-Violence-as-Armed-Conflict.pdf.

[18] Kevin Sieff, "Soldiers around the world get a new mission: Enforcing coronavirus lockdown." *Washington Post*. 25 March 2020, https://www.washingtonpost.com/world/

coronavirus-military-enforce-soldiers-armed-forces/2020/03/25/647cbbb6-6d53-11ea-a156-0048b62cdb51_story.html.

[19] This type of humanitarian diplomacy is a difficult but essential component of protecting the populace in areas faced with civil strife and extreme criminal violence bordering on or transcending the threshold of non-international armed conflicts (NIACs). See Robert Muggah and John P. Sullivan, "The Coming Crime Wars." *Foreign Policy*. 21 September 2018, https://foreignpolicy.com/2018/09/21/the-coming-crime-wars/; specifically germane to this pandemic, see Marcos Kotlik and Ezequil Heffes, "COVID-19 Symposium: COVID-19 in Conflict-Affected Areas–Armed Groups as Part of a Global Solution." *Opinio Juris*. 4 April 2020, http://opiniojuris.org/2020/04/04/covid-19-symposium-covid-19-in-conflict-affected-areas-armed-groups-as-part-of-a-global-solution/; and "Supporting COVID-19 response through the engagement of armed non-State actors." *Geneva Call*. 17 April 2020, https://www.genevacall.org/supporting-covid-19-response-by-the-engagement-of-armed-non-state-actors/.

For Additional Reading

Juan Ricardo Gómez Hecht, "Gangs in El Salvador: A New Type of Insurgency?" *Small Wars Journal*, 27 October 2017.

Juan Ricardo Gómez Hecht, "Las Pandillas en El Salvador: ¿Un Nuevo Tipo de Insurgencia?" *Small Wars Journal*, 4 September 2017.

John P. Sullivan, José de Arimatéia da Cruz and Robert J. Bunker, "Third Generation Gangs Strategic Note No. 22: Rio's Gangs Impose Curfews in Response to Coronavirus." *Small Wars Journal*, 10 April 2020.

John P. Sullivan and Robert J. Bunker, Eds. *Strategic Notes on Third Generation Gangs*. A Small Wars Journal-El Centro Anthology. Bloomington: Xlibris, 2020.

Chapter 3

Mexican Cartel Strategic Note No. 29: An Overview of Cartel Activities Related to COVID-19 Humanitarian Response

Robert J. Bunker and John P. Sullivan

First Published in Small Wars Journal on 8 May 2020

Various organized crime entities throughout Latin America, Europe, and Africa—including gangs, cartels, and mafias—are increasingly responding to the global COVID-19 pandemic in a number of ways. These include accounting for a shift in their illicit revenue streams and exploring new economic opportunities that are emerging. In the area of humanitarian response, a large number of the Mexican cartels are now actively engaging in these activities for their public relations and propaganda value in supporting their 'protector of the community narratives' targeted at the local citizenry under their control. These cartel activities are not without precedent and have taken place in Mexico in the past—though not as widespread and pronounced as they are now—and further reinforce ongoing criminal insurgency analysis related to this phenomena linked to Eric Hobsbawm's 'social banditry' construct.

Key Information: Drazen Joric, "El Chapo's daughter, Mexican cartels hand out coronavirus aid." Reuters. 16 April 2020, https://www.reuters.com/article/us-health-coronavirus-mexico-cartels/el-chapos-daughter-mexican-cartels-hand-out-coronavirus-aid-idUSKBN21Y3J7?utm_source=twitter&utm_medium=Social:

> MEXICO CITY (Reuters) - A daughter of famed drug lord Joaquin "El Chapo" Guzman and several Mexican cartels have been doling out aid packages to help cash-strapped residents ride out the coronavirus pandemic.

In one video posted on Facebook, Guzman's daughter, Alejandrina, can be seen stuffing toilet paper and food into a cardboard box bearing slick logos and a designer stencil-style image of her father, the former Sinaloa cartel chief who is now in a maximum security U.S. prison.

The oil, sugar, rice and other items in the boxes, which the video narrator calls "Chapo's provisions", were distributed in Mexico's second largest city, Guadalajara, in western Jalisco state.

Alejandrina's handout was linked to her company, which legally markets clothing and alcohol associated with her father's image under the "El Chapo 701" brand.

Key Information: "Reportan entrega de despensas del Cártel del Golfo en Ciudad Victoria, Tamaulipas." *Economía Hoy*. 6 April 2020. https://www.economiahoy.mx/nacional-eAm-mx/noticias/10466405/04/20/Reportan-entrega-de-despensas-del-Cartel-del-Golfo-en-Ciudad-Victoria-Tamaulipas.html:

> Usuarios de redes sociales difundieron este fin de semana fotografías en las que presuntos integrantes del **Cártel del Golfo (CDG)** entregaban cajas con despensa a pobladores de Ciudad Victoria, Tamaulipas como "apoyo" ante la pandemia de coronavirus.
>
> De acuerdo con las fotografías, en las cajas se puede leer la leyenda "Cártel del Golfo en apoyo a CD. Victoria. Señor 46 Vaquero".
>
> Cada caja contenía artículos como aceite, arroz, harina de maríz, latas de atún, galletas, cereal, azúcar, café, sopas y leche condensada.
>
> Según el conteo oficial, en Tamaulipas se han registrado 38 pacientes positivos de coronavirus y dos fallecimientos.
>
> Esta no es la primera vez que ocurre algo así. En 2013, cuando el Huracán Ingrid arrasó con la entidad, los damnificados también recibieron paquetes con alimentos por parte del mismo grupo cr[i]minal.

Note—*the article contains CDG social media (Twitter) postings with imagery.*

Key Information: "Los Viagras y el Cártel del Golfo: qué cárteles se están aprovechando del coronavirus para repartir despensas." *Infobae*. 7 April 2020, https://www.infobae.com/america/mexico/2020/04/07/los-viagras-y-el-cartel-del-golfo-que-carteles-se-estan-aprovechando-del-coronavirus-para-repartir-despensas/:

> El grupo criminal **Los Viagras** tienen mil y un rostros. Uno por cada persona que lo mira. En Michoacán es considerado un cártel "benefactor".
>
> Aprovechando la crisis por **coronavirus**, el grupo de narcotráfico, que ha logrado desordenar todo el estado, repartió decenas de despensas a los pobladores de la **comunidad de Acahuato, municipio de Apatzingán.**
>
> Un video revelado por *Breitbart News* muestra a hombres armados en una camioneta pick up con la batea llena de despensas.
>
> La grabación registra alrededor de 300 pobladores de la región recibir los insumos por parte de **"El Señor de la Virgen"**. "De la mera gente de la Virgen les vienen a regalar una despensa a cada uno. Son los que mandan aquí", dice uno de los sujetos.
>
> En Apatzingán y otros municipios de **Tierra Caliente** todos los días suceden robos de tráileres que transportan abarrotes hasta alimentos del campo. En la ciudad de Buenavista por ejemplo, los comerciantes y productores del campo son obligados a comprar a la delincuencia el producto de sus robos.

Note—*the article contains Los Viagras social media video posting screenshots.*

Key Information: "CJNG reparte despensa por coronavirus ahora en San Luis Potosí." *La Verdad Noticias*. 14 April 2020, https://laverdadnoticias.com/crimen/CJNG-reparte-despensa-por-coronavirus-ahora-en-San-Luis-Potosi-20200414-0033.html:

> De nueva cuenta sicarios del **Cártel Jalisco Nueva Generación (CJNG)** fueron vistos entregando **despensas** a los pobladores, aunque en esta ocasión en varias rancherías de **San Luis Potosí**…
>
> Aprovechando esta situación diversos grupos criminales, entre ellos el CJNG, han aprovechado la oportunidad para congraciarse con la población de diferentes municipios, pues se les ha visto llevando cajas con despensa a los pobladores que se han visto afectados por el coronavirus (Covid-19)…
>
> En esta ocasión los sicarios del CJNG entregaron la despensa en Salinas de Hidalgo, Villa de Arriaga, Villa de Reyes, Santa María del Río, Tierra Nueva, Rioverde, Villa de Zaragoza y Soledad de Graciano Sánchez.
>
> *Note—the article contains CJNG social media imagery.*

Key Information: "La Familia Michoacana también hace entrega de despensas ante el COVID-19." *La Verdad Noticias.* 19 April 2020, https://laverdadnoticias.com/crimen/La-Familia-Michoacana-tambien-hace-entrega-de-despensas-ante-el-COVID-19-20200419-0078.html:

> Ahora, para no quedarse atrás en la carrera, **La Familia Michoacana** no se quedó con las ganas de ayudar a los habitantes más necesitados y vulnerables, así que se unió a los otros cárteles regalando **despensas** ante la crisis sanitaria ocasionada por el **COVID-19**…
>
> Fue a través de redes sociales que esta organización criminal difundió las imágenes donde se puede observar a adultos mayores sosteniendo bolsas con despensas que contienen productos de la canasta básica, como productos enlatados, papel higiénico, cereales y cloro.
>
> Con la leyenda: "Apoyo de La Familia Michoacana. El comando de la M", las despensas fueron entregadas aunadas a una calcomanía pegada con las imágenes de un pescado y una fresa, haciendo referencia a los hermanos Hurtado Olascoaga.

> Los reportes oficiales indican que las despensas repartidas por sicarios de La Familia Michoacana fueron entregadas en los municipios de San Lucas, Villa Guerrero y Santiago en el sur del Estado de México, así como en localidades del municipio de Arcelia en Guerrero.

Analysis

Transnational gangs, criminal cartels, and mafias are adapting to and exploiting the COVID-19 pandemic in a variety of ways. These responses vary among jurisdictions and organizations.[1] In Rio de Janeiro, we see gangs (*gangues*) and militias (*milícias*) competing with each other and the state for competitive control of *favelas*.[2] In Cape Town, South Africa, rival gangs have instituted a truce and provide food parcels to the community.[3] In El Salvador, *maras* control social distancing while mafias in Italy and beyond seek to gain profit from the pandemic.[4] In Latin America, gangs—especially territorial-prison gang complexes—are gaining in strength and stature from opportunities provided by the COIVID-19 pandemic.[5]

In Mexico, the criminal cartel response to COVID-19 varies among cartels and the areas they control (or seek to control). In Sinaloa, the Sinaloa Cartel (CDS) faction dominated by Joaquín 'El Chapo' Guzmán Loera's family is providing humanitarian aid to the community and branding that aid with El Chapo's image.[6] In Tamaulipas, the Gulf cartel (CDG) is also distributing humanitarian aid in response to the pandemic.[7]

As Falko Ernst and Vanda Felbab Brown have observed, the provision of humanitarian aid by armed non-state actors (ANSAs) or criminal armed groups (CAGs) is not new.[8] The COVID-19 pandemic is just the latest iteration of a long-standing practice of the 'utilitarian provision of social goods' by rebels, and CAGs.

Derived from fragmentary social media postings and news reports the following Mexican cartel activities vis-à-vis the COVID-19 pandemic are provided on a cartel-by-cartel basis:

- **Cártel del Golfo**; CDG (Gulf Cartel): Hundreds of aid boxes were passed out to lower socio-economic residents in Ciudad Victoria and Matamoros, Tamaulipas by the Gulf Cartel. The boxes came in two different varieties—white cardboard boxes for Ciudad Victoria and brown cardboard boxes Matamoros. The boxes contained basic staples such as sugar, coffee, soups, oil, rice, cornmeal, tuna, crackers, cereal, and condensed milk. The boxes, of which over a hundred were delivered, were labeled so that the local residents knew that they were COVID-19 aid originating from the cartel rather than from the Mexican state or federal government. Each box had a sticker on it stating that it came from Señor 46 Vaquero—Evaristo "Comandante Vaquero" Cruz—the current CDG leader of the cartel faction running Matamoros. Photo opportunities of CDG gunmen standing next to the residents being provided with the boxes were widely taken in a number of instances and posted to social media by the cartel.[9] The cartel had earlier provided aid after Hurricane Ingrid took place in September 2013 in Tamaulipas and again in September 2017 after an earthquake affected a number of states.[10]

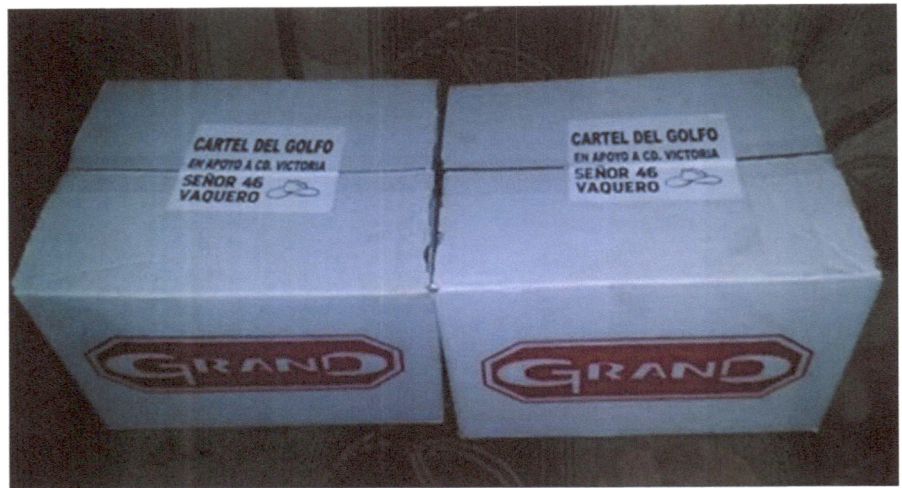

"Cartel del Golfo, en apoyo a CD. Victoria, Señor 46 Vaquero"

Source: Gulf Cartel Social Media. Reposted by La Expansion Chiapas. *Facebook*. 5 April 2020, https://www.facebook.com/photo.php?fbid=647989252701897&set=pcb.647989576035198&type=3&theater.

"Gulf Cartel gunmen posing with supplies provided to a local resident in Ciudad Victoria, Tamaulipas." Source: Gulf Cartel social media [*Twitter* post], 10 April 2020, https://twitter.com/vigilantehuaste/status/1249005928575152128/photo/3.

- **_Cártel de Sinaloa_**; CDS (Sinaloa Cartel); El Chapo's (Chapo Guzman's) Daughter: *Cártel de Sinaloa* has been linked to COVID-19 response activities on two levels. The first is on a humanitarian level and tangentially linked to CDS by means of El Chapo's daughter Alejandrina Guzman. She recently appeared in a video in Guadalajara providing 'Chapo Provisions' (*Chapo dispensas*) to local residents. These provisions consist of cardboard boxes filled with toilet paper, water, various food items such as soup and rice and beans, and soap. They are being provided as a publicity stunt for the El Chapo 701 fashion line tied to the commercial website https://www.elchapoguzman.com which is printed on the side of the cardboard boxes with his image. The young ladies providing the provisions sport El Chapo facemasks with a shirt from the clothing line also evident in part of the video.[11] More closely linked to CDS are provisions being given to local residents in Santa Bárbara, Chihuahua by *la Gente Nueva*; GN (the New People) who are the armed wing of the cartel. Hundreds of packages in plastic bags sporting the image of Osama bin Laden were delivered to the poor and older individuals in the community. The provisions included soap, chlorine, toilet paper, maseca, oatmeal, sugar, coffee, soups and other canned goods.[12] The second level of activities linking CDS to COVID-19 response is via quarantine enforcement. In a video released by CDS, a wooden paddle labeled 'COVID 19' is being utilized by Sinaloa cartel *sicarios* (hitmen) to spank the bare buttocks of an individual who ignored the curfew enacted by *Los Chapitos* (El Chapo's sons). The curfew does not apply to people going or returning from work during the day and into the evening but is in full force after 10:00 pm for all individuals.[13]

Alejandrina Guzman filling a 'Chapo Provision.'

Source: Newsflash/@elchapoguzmanoficial701 Social Media Marketing.

Reposted by ViralTab, https://viraltab.news/el-chapo-covid-masks-as-daughter-distributes-aid-boxes/.

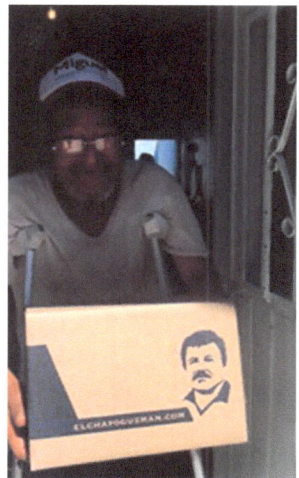

Elderly handicapped resident in Guadalajara receiving a 'Chapo Provision.'

Source: Newsflash/@elchapoguzmanoficial701 Social Media Marketing. Reposted by ViralTab, https://viraltab.news/el-chapo-covid-masks-as-daughter-distributes-aid-boxes/.

Older Women in Santa Bárbara, Chihuahua Receiving Relief Package from Armed Gente Nueva Gunman. Source: CDS Social Media Posted at WhatsApp.

Reprinted in *Infobae*, https://www.infobae.com/america/mexico/2020/04/24/presuntos-integra…loa-repartieron-despensas-en-chihuahua-con-la-imagen-de-bin-laden/.

Resident in Sinaloa Having Bare Buttocks Paddled by CDS Hitman

Source: CDS Social Media Twitter Video Posting (Screen Shot at 0 Seconds of 38 Second Video)"VIDEO - Chapitos Sicarios del Cártel de Sinaloa lo levantan y tablean por no respetar sus ordenes de no salir por COVID-19." *Frontera Al Rojo Vivo*. 19 April 2020, https://lare2s.blogspot.com/2020/04/video-chapitos-sicarios-del-cartel-de.html?utm_source=dlvr.it&utm_medium=twitter.

- ***La Familia Michoacana***; LFM, FM (The Michoacán Family—Remnant 'El Comando de la M'): *La Familia* leaders Jhony "El Mojarro" and José "La Fresa" Hurtado Olascoaga (who are related) provided COVID-19 aid to low income and older residents in San Lucas, Villa Guerrero, and Santiago in southern Mexico as well as towns in the municipality of Arcelia, Guerrero. The aid consisted of plastic bags containing toilet paper, chlorine, canned goods, and cereal with a sticker attached stating "Apoyo de La Familia Michoacana, El Comando de La 'M'" (Support from La Familia Michoacana, The M Command). The sticker also had a Fish and Strawberry on it. These are the symbols of the Hurtado Olascoaga brothers.[14] For a video containing images of heavily armed FM forces and its gunmen (*sicarios*) handing out the provisions see the following cartel social media reposted at *YouTube*.[15] *La Familia Michoacana* as well as its successor *Los Caballeros Templarios de Michoacán* (The Knights Templar of Michoacán)—unlike most of the Mexican cartels—has a long tradition of "more extensive and formalized efforts at service provision" rather than engaging in opportunistic aid activities for solely propagandistic purposes.[16] The FM El Comando de La

'M' faction of the cartel is a marginal group and relatively minor in importance compared to the organization's strength during its height quite a few years ago.

COVID-19 Aid Package with the Sticker "Apoyo de La Familia Michoacana, El Comando de La 'M'" with a Fish and a Strawberry Image (Translated: Support from La Familia Michoacana, The M Command; The Fish and Strawberry are the symbols of the Hurtado Olascoaga brothers who are LFM leaders). Source: LFM Social Media.

Reposted at *La Verdad Noticias*, https://laverdadnoticias.com/crimen/La-Familia-Michoacana-tambien-hace-entrega-de-despensas-ante-el-COVID-19-20200419-0078.html.

- ***Cártel de Jalisco Nueva Generación***; CJNG (Jalisco New Generation Cartel): The cartel has been has been giving out COVID-19 aid to residents in the municipalities of Salinas de Hidalgo, Villa de Arriga, Villa de Reyes, Santa María del Río, Tierra Nueva, Rioverde, Villa de Zaragoza, and Soledad de Graciano Sánchez in San Luis Potosí[17] and earlier in Cuautitlán, Jalisco[18]. In the case of Cuautitlán, one or more caravans of CJNG vehicles with supplies for the local inhabitants were said to have entered the area. The provisions were given on behalf of Nemesio Oseguera Cervantes 'El Mencho' the leader of CJNG under his other pseudonym 'El Señor de los Gallos' (The Lord of the Roosters).[19] The aid is being provided as free gifts to win over the local communities by attempting to convince them that CJNG is with the people and is their friend.

'El Señor de los Gallos, Mencho, Con El Pueblo' (The Lord of the Roosters, El Mencho; Leader of the CJNG, with the people) Poster in San Luis Potosí. Source: CJNG Social Media Posting. Reprinted in *Vanguardia,* https://vanguardia.com.mx/articulo/cartel-de-jalisco-regala-despensas-por-coronavirus-de-parte-de-el-mencho.

COVID-19 Provisions Provided to Local Residents

The Sticker on the Box Reads 'De parte de sus amigos, apoyo por contingencia COVID-19' (From your friends, COVID-19 contingency support)

Source: CJNG Social Media Posting. Reprinted in *Daily Mail,* https://www.dailymail.co.uk/news/article-8218479/Notorious-Mexican-cartels-aid-countrys-poor-struggling-coronavirus-pandemic.html.

- ***Los Viagras*** (The Viagras): The *Los Viagras* cartel has been identified as passing out COVID-19 aid in the form of food to hundreds of residents in the region of the municipalities of Apatzingán[20] and Santiago Acahuato[21], Michoacán. *Cártel de Jalisco Nueva Generación* is dominant in this region with the food aid being used to undermine their authority and bring community goodwill to *Los Viagras*[22]. Part of this aid is said to be funded by street taxation (*renta*) of local businesses:

    "Sources close to Los Viagras, the group that recorded its hand-outs in the streets of Apatzingán, said the group is asking local businesses for 'contributions' to finance its aid."[23]

    Los Viagras Passing Out Food to Community Members in the Apatzingán region of Michoacán. Source: Las Viagras Social Media Video Posting on WhatsApp.

    Reposted in "Cartels take advantage of Covid-19 to 'buy' population and territory with food aid." *Plataforma*. 21 April 2020, https://www.plataformamedia.com/en-uk/news/society/cartels-take-advantage-of-covid-19-to-buy-population-and-territory-with-food-aid-12097422.html.

- ***Los Zetas*** (Zetas Cartel Remnant): COVID-19 aid has been passed out by Commander 45 Z in Coatzacoalcos, Veracruz, which is a major port city in its southern region. The aid consisting of toilet paper and other household goods is provided in clear basic bags with a sticker attached stating "En apoyo a la ciudadana de Coatzacoalcos y sas Alrededores de parte Del SR COMANDANTE Z45" along with a shield with some non-distinct images on it. The text is translated to read "In support of the citizens of Coatzacoalcos and surroundings on behalf of Commander Z45." The reporting on this aid is fragmentary and drawn from what appears to be cartel related social media:

Source: Ignacio Carvajal's *Facebook* Page. Reposted by Código Veracruz Noticias. 16 April 2020, https://www.facebook.com/CodigoVeracruzNoticias/posts/2590548131267420.

Residents of Receiving COVID-19 Aid from Commander 45 Z in Coatzacoalcos, Veracruz. Source: Ignacio Carvajal's *Facebook* Page. Reposted by Código Veracruz Noticias. 16 April 2020, https://www.facebook.com/CodigoVeracruzNoticias/posts/2590548131267420.

- **Los Grandos** (Beltrán Leyva Organization; BLO Remnant): Two video postings—one via social media[24] and one via a television broadcast[25]—showing the image of a man being struck on the buttocks with a stick with a line of other men awaiting their discipline for ignoring a local curfew put in place by a criminal organization in Teloloapan, Guerrero have been identified.[26]

Resident Being Disciplined for Breaking Curfew in Teloloapan, Guerrero by Undetermined Cartel. Social Media. Buggs @alexmarentes. *Twitter*, 24 April 2020, https://twitter.com/alexmarentes/status/1253773933188284416.

CARTEL & SYMBOL	LOCATION	ACTIVITIES ENGAGED IN
Cártel del Golfo; CDG (Gulf Cartel)	Ciudad Victoria & Matamoros, Tamaulipas	• Provision of Aid
Cártel de Sinaloa; CDS (Sinaloa Cartel); El Chapo's Daughter (El Chapo 701 Brand)	Guadalajara, Jalisco (701 Brand; Aid) Santa Bárbara, Chihuahua ('Gente Nueva' or 'New People' Armed CDS Wing; Aid) Unspecified CDS territories in Sinaloa (Quarantine)	• Provision of Aid • Quarantine Enforcement
La Familia Michoacána; FM (The Michoacan Family—Remnant 'El Comando de la M')	San Lucas, Villa Guerrero and Santiago in southern Mexico. Towns in the municipality of Arcelia, Guerrero	• Provision of Aid

Table 1a. Mexican Cartel Activities Related to COVID-19

CARTEL & SYMBOL	LOCATION	ACTIVITIES ENGAGED IN
Cártel de Jalisco Nueva Generación; CJNG (Jalisco New Generation Cartel)	Salinas de Hidalgo, Villa de Arriga, Villa de Reyes, Santa María del Río, Tierra Nueva, Rioverde, Villa de Zaragoza, and Soledad de Graciano Sánchez in San Luis Potosí Cuautitlán, Jalisco	• Provision of Aid
Los Viagras (The Viagras)	Apatzingán and Santiago Acahuato region, Michoacán	• Provision of Aid • COVID-19 Street Tax
Los Zetas— Remnant Under 45 Z	Coatzacoalcos, Veracruz	• Provision of Aid
Los Grandos— Beltrán Leyva Organization; BLO Remnant	Teloloapan, Guerrero	• Quarantine Enforcement

Table 1b. Mexican Cartel Activities Related to COVID-19

The preceding activities engaged in by the Mexican cartels related to COVID-19 have been summarized in Table 1a&b.[27] Three types of activities have been identified—the provision of aid to the community, special taxing of businesses to provide that aid, and quarantine (social distancing or curfew) enforcement. The special taxing appears to be a one-off activity conducted by *Los Viagras* either due to organizational greed or their lack of economic capacity to provide aid to local residents which seems less likely. What has been more typical—at least from that of some of the *maras* in El Salvador—has been some street tax forgiveness due to the economic hardships COVID-19 has been causing. The La Unión Tepito criminal group in Mexico City, however, is collecting its extortion payments from local businesses like small shops and street sellers.[28] Quarantine enforcement of the local populace in the case of the *Cártel de Sinaloa* 'Gente Nueva' wing and *Los Grandos* in Mexico is a more common activity and has been evident in other criminal organizations in Brazil[29] and Central America[30].

The actual provision of aid to the local populace appears to be more of a Mexican Cartel phenomenon—as opposed to the *maras* and other criminal entities in Latin America. It is most evident with cartel *plaza jefes* (city bosses) and cartel *jefes* who are having their names and organizational imagery (*i.e.* criminal branding) directly linked to the provision of COVID-19 aid, such as Señor 46 Vaquero in Cuidad Victoria and Matamoros (CDG), El Chapo in Guadalajara (CDS; via his daughter), the Hurtado Olascoaga brothers in various towns in southern Mexico and Guerrero (FM), El Mencho in the states of San Luis Potosí and Jalisco (CJNG), and Commander 45 Z in Coatzacoalcos (Zetas remnant).[31] This is in line with Hobsbawm's writings on 'social banditry' embodied in his works *Bandits* (1969) and reflected in our recent SWJ-El Centro anthology *The Rise of the Narco State* (2019)[32]. The *plaza jefes* are attempting to undermine the state in the eyes of the local residents for its unjust feudal (e.g. authoritarian) treatment of them. Tied to a 'Robin Hood' archetype, they seek to become the underclasses' benefactor for public goods and, as a result, gain their loyalty and trust. However, in many instances, such aid attempts are primitive in nature with the local residents highly fearful of not appearing grateful enough in their acceptance given that it is being delivered by heavily armed cartel *sicarios* (gunmen).[33]

Still, the high level of publicity surrounding the delivery of this aid—especially after the El Chapo 701 fashion line media stunt in Guadalajara—has gotten the full attention of the highest levels of Mexican federal authority. This has resulted in Mexican President Andrés Manuel López Obrador (AMLO) stating that the criminal organization provision of "care packages filled with basic foodstuffs and cleaning supplies were not helpful."[34]

The Coronavirus, COVID-19 pandemic has exposed the underlying tensions between states and their criminal competitors. Criminal cartels and territorial gangs (Third Generation Gangs) are actively competing with the state and providing humanitarian aid and exerting informal social control to secure support from the communities where they operate. This competition is an indicator of state transition (or state-making) utilizing the mantle of 'social banditry' as described by Hobsbawm and Sullivan.[35] Future research and experience is needed to determine the long-term effects of this humanitarian branding within cartel-controlled areas and in relation to the state at large.

Sources

Drazen Joric, "El Chapo's daughter, Mexican cartels hand out coronavirus aid." Reuters. 16 April 2020, https://www.reuters.com/article/us-health-coronavirus-mexico-cartels/el-chapos-daughter-mexican-cartels-hand-out-coronavirus-aid-idUSKBN21Y3J7?utm_source=twitter&utm_medium=Social.

"Reportan entrega de despensas del Cártel del Golfo en Ciudad Victoria, Tamaulipas (Reports of a delivery of pantry items by the Gulf Cartel in Ciudad Victoria, Tamaulipas)." *Economía Hoy*. 6 April 2020, https://www.economiahoy.mx/nacional-eAm-mx/noticias/10466405/04/20/Reportan-entrega-de-despensas-del-Cartel-del-Golfo-en-Ciudad-Victoria-Tamaulipas.html.

"Los Viagras y el Cártel del Golfo: qué cárteles se están aprovechando del coronavirus para repartir despensas." *Infobae*. 7 April 2020, https://www.infobae.com/america/mexico/2020/04/07/los-viagras-y-el-cartel-del-golfo-que-carteles-se-estan-aprovechando-del-coronavirus-para-repartir-despensas/.

"CJNG reparte despensa por coronavirus ahora en San Luis Potosí." *La Verdad Noticias*.14 April 2020, https://laverdadnoticias.com/crimen/CJNG-reparte-despensa-por-coronavirus-ahora-en-San-Luis-Potosi-20200414-0033.html.

"La Familia Michoacana también hace entrega de despensas ante el COVID-19." *La Verdad Noticias*. 19 April 2020, https://laverdadnoticias.com/crimen/La-Familia-Michoacana-tambien-hace-entrega-de-despensas-ante-el-COVID-19-20200419-0078.html

Endnotes

[1] See Richard Behar, "Organized Crime in the Time of Corona." *Forbes*. 27 March 2020, https://www.forbes.com/sites/richardbehar/2020/03/27/organized-crime-in-the-time-of-corona/#4c2725f0150d; Kevin

Sieff, Susannah George, and Kareem Fahim, "Now Joining the Fight Against Coronavirus: The World's Armed Rebels, Drug Cartels and Gangs." *Washington Post*. 14 April 2020, https://www.washingtonpost.com/world/the_americas/coronavirus-taliban-ms-13-drug-cartels-gangs/2020/04/13/83aa07ac-79c2-11ea-a311-adb1344719a9_story.html; Colin P. Clarke, "Yesterday's Terrorists Are Today's Public-Health Providers." *Foreign Policy*. 8 April 2020, https://foreignpolicy.com/2020/04/08/terrorists-nonstate-ungoverned-health-providers-coronavirus-pandemic/; and "Crime and Contagion: The impact of a pandemic on organized Crime." Policy Brief. Global Initiative Against Transnational Crime. March 2020, https://globalinitiative.net/wp-content/uploads/2020/03/CovidPB1rev.04.04.v1.pdf. In addition, an emerging research project at Indications for Poverty Action is assessing the variations in gang and organized crime reaction in Medellín, Colombia to the COVID-19 pandemic. See Christopher Blattman, Benjamin Lessing, Santiago Tobon, Gustavo Duncan, "The Other Virus: How Gangs and Organized Crime are Responding to the COVID-19 Crisis." IPA (Indications for Poverty Action), https://www.poverty-action.org/recovr-study/other-virus-how-gangs-and-organized-crime-are-responding-covid-19-crisis.

[2] See Niko Vorobyov, "Inside the Gangs Handing Out Pandemic Supplies in Rio's Favelas. Filter. 27 April 2020, https://filtermag.org/rio-gangs-favelas-coronavirus/ and John P. Sullivan, José de Arimatéia da Cruz and Robert J. Bunker, "Third Generation Gangs Strategic Note No. 22: Rio's Gangs Impose Curfews in Response to Coronavirus." *Small Wars Journal*. 10 April 2020, https://smallwarsjournal.com/jrnl/art/third-generation-gangs-strategic-note-no-22-rios-gangs-impose-curfews-response-coronavirus.

[3] Peta Thornycroft, "Unprecedented truce in notorious South African slums as gangs join forces to hand out coronavirus aid." *The Telegraph*. 12 April 2020, https://www.telegraph.co.uk/news/2020/04/12/unprecedented-truce-notorious-south-african-slums-gangs-join/.

[4] See John P. Sullivan, Robert J. Bunker and Juan Ricardo Gómez Hecht, "Third Generation Gangs Strategic Note No. 23: El Salvadoran Gangs (Maras) Enforce Domestic Quarantine / Stay at Home Orders (Cuarentena domiciliar)." *Small Wars Journal*. 5 May 2020, https://smallwarsjournal.com/jrnl/art/third-generation-gangs-strategic-note-no-23-el-salvadoran-gangs-maras-enforce-domestic and Valantina Di Donato and Tim Lister, "The Mafia is poised to exploit coronavirus, and not just in Italy. CNN (at *WTOP News*). 19 April 2020, https://wtop.com/coronavirus/2020/04/the-mafia-is-poised-to-exploit-coronavirus-and-not-just-in-italy/.

[5] See Steven Dudley, "Latin America's Prison Gangs Draw Strength From the Pandemic." *Foreign Affairs*. 5 May 2020, https://www.foreignaffairs.com/articles/americas/2020-05-05/latin-americas-prison-gangs-draw-strength-pandemic; John P. Sullivan, "The Challenges of Territorial Gangs: Civil Strife, Criminal

Insurgencies and Crime Wars." *Revista do Ministério Público Militar* (Brazil), Edição n. 31, November 2019, https://www.academia.edu/40917684/The_Challenges_of_Territorial_Gangs_Civil_Strife_Criminal_Insurgencies_and_Crime_Wars; and Vanda Felbab-Brown and Paul Wise, "When pandemics come to slums." *Brookings*. 6 April 2020, https://www.brookings.edu/blog/order-from-chaos/2020/04/06/when-pandemics-come-to-slums/.

[6] Drazen Joric, "El Chapo's daughter, Mexican cartels hand out coronavirus aid." Reuters. 16 April 2020, https://www.reuters.com/article/us-health-coronavirus-mexico-cartels/el-chapos-daughter-mexican-cartels-hand-out-coronavirus-aid-idUSKBN21Y3J7?utm_source=twitter&utm_medium=Social.

[7] "Reportan entrega de despensas del Cártel del Golfo en Ciudad Victoria, Tamaulipas." *Economía Hoy*. 6 April 2020. https://www.economiahoy.mx/nacional-eAm-mx/noticias/10466405/04/20/Reportan-entrega-de-despensas-del-Cartel-del-Golfo-en-Ciudad-Victoria-Tamaulipas.html.

[8] See Falko Ernst, "Mexican criminal groups see Covid-19 crisis as opportunity to gain more power." *The Guardian*. 20 April 2020, https://www.theguardian.com/world/2020/apr/20/mexico-criminal-groups-covid-19-crisis-opportunity-gain-power and Vanda Felbab-Brown, "Mexican cartels are providing COVID-19 assistance. Why that's not surprising." *Brookings*. 27 April 2020, https://www.brookings.edu/blog/order-from-chaos/2020/04/27/mexican-cartels-are-providing-covid-19-assistance-why-thats-not-surprising/.

[9] Alma Keshavaraz and Robert J. Bunker, "Gulf Cartel Distributes Food and Supplies to Residents of Ciudad Victoria, Tamaulipas." *OE Watch*. May 2020: 88. See also Fernando Eslava, "Cártel del Golfo reparte despensas en Tamaulipas por Covid-19." *La Hoguera*. 6 April 2020. https://lahoguera.mx/cartel-del-golfo-reparte-despensas-en-tamaulipas-por-covid-19/; "Cartel del Golfo reparte despensas a familias de escasos recursos ante la contingencia de Coronavirus." *MTP Noticias*. 6 April 2020. https://mtpnoticias.com/viral/virales/cartel-del-golfo-reparte-despensas-a-familias-de-escasos-recursos-ante-la-contingencia-de-coronavirus/; and "Mexican Cartel Gunmen Distribute Food Baskets Amid Coronavirus, Easter." Cartel Chronicles. *Breitbart*. 14 April 2020, https://www.breitbart.com/border/2020/04/14/mexican-cartel-gunmen-distribute-food-baskets-amid-coronavirus-easter/.

[10] John P. Sullivan, "Criminal Insurgency: Narcocultura, Social Banditry, and Information Operations." *Small Wars Journal*. 3 December 2012, Mexican Cartel Strategic Note No. 15: Skullduggery or Social Banditry? Cartel Humanitarian Aid and John P. Sullivan and Robert J. Bunker, "Mexican Cartel Strategic Note No. 24: Cartel and Gang Provision of Post-Earthquake

Humanitarian Aid." *Small Wars Journal*. 21 October 2017, https://smallwarsjournal.com/jrnl/art/mexican-cartel-strategic-note-no-24-cartel-and-gang-provision-post-earthquake-humanitarian.

[11] Ana Lacasa, "El Chapo COVID Masks As Daughter Distributes Aid Boxes." ViralTab. 22 April 2020, https://viraltab.news/el-chapo-covid-masks-as-daughter-distributes-aid-boxes/. The story is generated by NewsFlash a 'bespoke agency' who generate news media—presumably for the El Chapo 701 line in this instance—for marketing purposes. See also Adry Torres, "El Chapo's daughter films herself loading up food packages that have the drug lord's face printed on them for the elderly struggling in Mexico during the coronavirus pandemic." *Daily Mail*. 16 April 2020, https://www.dailymail.co.uk/news/article-8227469/El-Chapos-daughter-prepares-boxes-food-supplies-elderly-struggling-COVID-19.html.

[12] "Presuntos integrantes del cártel de Sinaloa repartieron despensas en Chihuahua con la imagen de Bin Laden." *Infobae*. 24 April 2020, https://www.infobae.com/america/mexico/2020/04/24/presuntos-integra…loa-repartieron-despensas-en-chihuahua-con-la-imagen-de-bin-laden/.

[13] "VIDEO: Chapitos Sicarios del Cártel de Sinaloa lo levantan y tablean por no respetar sus ordenes de no salir por COVID-19." *Frontera Al Rojo Vivo*. 19 April 2020, https://lare2s.blogspot.com/2020/04/video-chapitos-sicarios-del-cartel-de.html?utm_source=dlvr.it&utm_medium=twitter.

[14] "La Familia Michoacana también hace entrega de despensas ante el COVID-19." *La Verdad Noticias*. 19 April 2020, https://laverdadnoticias.com/crimen/La-Familia-Michoacana-tambien-hace-entrega-de-despensas-ante-el-COVID-19-20200419-0078.html and "La Familia Michoacana se une al reparto de despensas." *Proceso*. 17 April 2020, https://www.proceso.com.mx/626282/la-familia-despensas.

[15] "La Familia Michoacana reparte despensas #Guerrero #Edomex." *YouTube*. 19 April 2020, https://www.google.com/url?sa=i&url=https%3A%2F%2Fwww.youtube.com%2Fwatch%3Fv%3DI-Fm4eY46d4&psig=AOvVaw2cMzIMfekUPglEeiROr2Tb&ust=1587858561263000&source=images&cd=vfe&ved=2ahUKEwjElKCdoILpAhWSlZ4KHTGqCPcQr4kDegQIARBK.

[16] Shawn T. Flanigan, "Motivations and Implications of Community Service Provision by La Familia Michoacána / Knights Templar and other Mexican Drug Cartels." *Journal of Strategic Security*. Vol. 7, No. 3, Fall 2014: 66, https://scholarcommons.usf.edu/cgi/viewcontent.cgi?article=1365&context=jss.

[17] "CJNG reparte despensa por coronavirus ahora en San Luis Potosí." *La Verdad Noticias*. 14 April 2020, https://laverdadnoticias.com/crimen/CJNG-reparte-despensa-por-coronavirus-ahora-en-San-Luis-

Potosi-20200414-0033.html. See also Adry Torres, "Notorious Mexican cartels hand out food and sanitizer to poor struggling with the coronavirus pandemic." *The Daily Mail*. 14 April 2020, https://www.dailymail.co.uk/news/article-8218479/Notorious-Mexican-cartels-aid-countrys-poor-struggling-coronavirus-pandemic.html.

[18] "CJNG hace entrega de despensas a pobladores de Cuautitlán." *La Verdad Noticias*. 10 April 2020, https://laverdadnoticias.com/crimen/CJNG-hace-entrega-de-despensas-a-pobladores-de-Cuautitlan-20200410-0203.html.

[19] CJNG hace entrega de despensas a pobladores de Cuautitlán." *La Verdad Noticias*.

[20] Falko Ernst, "Mexican criminal groups see Covid-19 crisis as opportunity to gain more power." *The Guardian*. 20 April 2020, https://www.theguardian.com/world/2020/apr/20/mexico-criminal-groups-covid-19-crisis-opportunity-gain-power.

[21] Laura Mallene, "Mexican Drug Cartel Gives Out Food to the Poor Amid Pandemic." Organized Crime and Corruption Reporting Project. 7 April 2020, https://www.occrp.org/en/daily/12038-mexican-drug-cartel-gives-out-food-to-the-poor-amid-pandemic. Originally sourced to information provided in "Integrantes de el Cartel del Golfo entrega despensas por Covid-19 en Tamaulipas." *El Blog Del Narco*. 5 April 2020, https://elblogdelnarco.com/2020/04/05/integrantes-de-el-cartel-del-golfo-entrega-despensas-por-covid-19-en-tamaulipas/.

[22] "Cartels take advantage of Covid-19 to 'buy' population and territory with food aid." *Plataforma*. 21 April 2020, https://www.plataformamedia.com/en-uk/news/society/cartels-take-advantage-of-covid-19-to-buy-population-and-territory-with-food-aid-12097422.html.

[23] Falko Ernst, "Mexican criminal groups see Covid-19 crisis as opportunity to gain more power."

[24] Social Media. Buggs @alexmarentes. *Twitter*. 24 April 2020, https://twitter.com/alexmarentes/status/1253773933188284416.

[25] Uno Video. TOMAS Munzer, Ocosingo Chiapas. *Facebook*. 20 April 2020, https://www.facebook.com/pg/TOMAS-Munzer-Ocosingo-Chiapas-1056036444438481/posts/.

[26] Cartel identification provided by Alex Marentes—owner and founder of *Borderland Beat*—who was informed by an anonymous source. *Twitter* communication with Buggs @alexmarentes on 27 April

2020, https://twitter.com/alexmarentes/status/1254943777589878784. City identification derived from *Facebook* posting by *Azteca Noticias* on 20 April 2020, https://bit.ly/2zgTVdQ [shortened URL]. For cartel background see, "Granados gang boss caught in Guerrero." *Mexico News Daily*. 13 April 2017, https://mexiconewsdaily.com/news/granados-gang-boss-caught-in-guerrero/.

[27] The Cártel de Santa Rosa de Lima (CSRL) has been said to been passing out COVID-19 aid in some news articles. See, for example, "La Familia Michoacana también hace entrega de despensas ante el COVID-19." *La Verdad Noticias*. 19 April 2020, https://laverdadnoticias.com/crimen/La-Familia-Michoacana-tambien-hace-entrega-de-despensas-ante-el-COVID-19-20200419-0078.html. No direct photographic evidence of such aid has been identified in online cartel social media or news reports specifically addressing it.

[28] Maria Alejandra Navarrete, "Extortion Payments in Mexico and Central America." *InSight Crime*. 13 April 2020, https://www.insightcrime.org/news/analysis/coronavirus-extortion-mexico-central-america/.

[29] John P. Sullivan, José de Arimatéia da Cruz and Robert J. Bunker, "Third Generation Gangs Strategic Note No. 22: Rio's Gangs Impose Curfews in Response to Coronavirus."

[30] John P. Sullivan, Robert J. Bunker and Juan Ricardo Gómez Hecht, "Third Generation Gangs Strategic Note No. 23: El Salvadoran Gangs (Maras) Enforce Domestic Quarantine / Stay at Home Orders (Cuarentena domiciliar)."

[31] In the case of *Los Viagras*, no *plaza jefe* has been identified as taking responsibility for the provision of aid to the local community.

[32] Eric Hobsbawm, *Bandits*. New York: Delacorte Press, 1969 and John P. Sullivan and Robert J. Bunker, Eds., *The Rise of the Narcostate (Mafia States)*. A Small Wars Journal-El Centro Anthology. Bloomington: Xlibris, 2018.

[33] A La Familia Michoacana member informed a journalist that "Ungrateful ones, will be killed" concerning their distribution of COVID-19 provisions to the local community. Chivis Martinez, Trans., "La Familia Michoacana debates journalist – 'We should be applauded' for Covid19 help 'Ungrateful ones, will be killed." *Borderland Beat*. 24 April 2020, http://www.borderlandbeat.com/2020/04/la-familia-michoacana-debates.html. Original Spanish source, "Falsas ayudas del crimen organizado a damnificados por COVID-19." *Nota de MVS Noticias*. 23 April 2020, https://mvsnoticias.com/videos/nacion-criminal/falsas-ayudas-del-crimen-organizado-a-damnificados-por-covid-19/.

[34] "Mexico president tells gangs to stop handing out coronavirus aid." *Al Jazeera*. 21 April 2020, https://www.aljazeera.com/news/2020/04/mexico-president-tells-gangs-stop-handing-coronavirus-aid-200421060420772.html.

[35] On state transition (and state-making), see Charles Tilly, "War Making and State Making as Organized Crime." Chapter 5 in Peter B. Evans, Dietrich Rueschemeyer, and Theda Skocpol, Eds. *Bringing the State Back In* (pp. 169-191). Cambridge: Cambridge University Press. doi:10.1017/CBO9780511628283.008. On social banditry, see Eric Hobsbawm, *Bandits*, at note 32 and John P. Sullivan, "Criminal Insurgency: Narcocultura, Social Banditry, and Information Operations" at note 10.

Additional Reading

Mexico Specific

Shawn T. Flanigan, "Motivations and Implications of Community Service Provision by La Familia Michoacána / Knights Templar and other Mexican Drug Cartels." *Journal of Strategic Security*. Vol. 7, No. 3, Fall 2014: 63-83.

John P. Sullivan, "Criminal Insurgency: Narcocultura, Social Banditry, and Information Operations." *Small Wars Journal*, 3 December 2012.

John P. Sullivan, "Mexican Cartel Strategic Note No. 15: Skullduggery or Social Banditry? Cartel Humanitarian Aid." *Small Wars Journal*, 25 November 2013.

John P. Sullivan and Robert J. Bunker, "Mexican Cartel Strategic Note No. 24: Cartel and Gang Provision of Post-Earthquake Humanitarian Aid." *Small Wars Journal*, 21 October 2017.

COVID-19 Specific

John P. Sullivan, José de Arimatéia da Cruz and Robert J. Bunker, "Third Generation Gangs Strategic Note No. 22: Rio's Gangs Impose Curfews in Response to Coronavirus." *Small Wars Journal*, 10 April 2020.

John P. Sullivan, Robert J. Bunker and Juan Ricardo Gómez Hecht, "Third Generation Gangs Strategic Note No. 23: El Salvadoran Gangs (Maras) Enforce Domestic Quarantine / Stay at Home Orders (Cuarentena domiciliar)." *Small Wars Journal,* 5 May 2020.

Chapter 4:

Third Generation Gangs Strategic Note No. 24: COVID-19, Gangs and Lockdown in Cape Town

John P. Sullivan and Robert J. Bunker

First Published in Small Wars Journal on 18 May 2020

Gangs in the Cape Town region have enacted a truce in the wake of the COVID-19 pandemic. South Africa is in the midst of a lockdown to contain the coronavirus outbreak that is also leading to food shortages. The truce involves gangs throughout the Cape Flats, including Manenberg. The participating gangs are joining together to distribute food, soap, and essential goods in an effort to provide relief to the communities in which they exist.[1]

South African Police Service (SAPS) Lockdown Checkpoint Source: SAPS, 3 May 2020, https://twitter.com/SAPoliceService/status/1256880475630682115?s=20.

Key Information: Peta Thornycroft, "Unprecedented truce in notorious South African slums as gangs join forces to hand out coronavirus aid." *The Telegraph*. 12 April 2020, https://www.telegraph.co.uk/news/2020/04/12/unprecedented-truce-notorious-south-african-slums-gangs-join/:

> It is being hailed as a miracle. In the face of a common enemy some of South Africa's most violent gangs have put down their knives and are working together to help their rivals cope with the coronavirus crisis.
>
> The gangs, until recently at each other's throats fighting for control of scarce resources in the poverty stricken suburbs of Cape Town, have begun to hand out food parcels to their former enemies.
>
> Organised by an investment banker turned church pastor, the initiative has seen the likes of convicted murderer Preston Jacobs, 35, distributing aid parcels in the deprived suburb of Manenberg, including to members of rival gangs.
>
> Mr Jacobs, leader of the long-established 'Americans' gang, who was released in 2018 from a seven-year jail sentence for his part in the death of a man from a rival gangs, now finds himself handing out food to members of gangs he used to hate…

Key Information: "'Literally a miracle': Violent rival gangs in South Africa call truce to help people during pandemic." *CBS News*. 18 April 2020, https://www.cbsnews.com/news/coronavirus-cape-town-violent-rival-gangs-south-africa-call-truce-pandemic/:

> Warring gangs in South Africa are working together in an unprecedented truce to deliver much-needed food to people under lockdown. The country has seen a 75% decrease in violent crime since it imposed strict restrictions over the coronavirus pandemic, and normally dangerous streets in Cape Town now see sworn enemies meeting up to collect essential goods to distribute throughout hungry communities.

Key Information: Tim Wyatt, "Coronavirus: Gang kingpins in South Africa call truce to help community during pandemic." *The Independent*. 20 April 2020, https://www.independent.co.uk/news/world/africa/south-africa-coronavirus-lockdown-gangs-cape-town-a9474101.html:

South Africa's coronavirus lockdown has unexpectedly brought warring gangs together to deliver food parcels to those struggling to make ends meet…

Across South Africa normally has some of the highest rates of violent crime in the whole continent but since the lockdown began has seen the numbers of murders, assaults and robberies collapse.

Some claim this is because gang leaders on the Council, a network of kingpins across South Africa, have collectively agreed to a ceasefire. Others, including the country's police minister Bheki Cele are credited the ban on liquor as well as a slump in demand for drugs which fuels gang activity.

Key Information: Loki Prinsloo and Pauline Bax, "How lockdown got gangs to declare truce amid dwindling drug sales." *Business Day*. 20 April 2020, https://www.businesslive.co.za/bd/national/2020-04-20-how-lockdown-got-gangs-to-declare-truce-amid-dwindling-drug-sales/:

Gangs in SA [South Africa], which has one of the world's highest homicide rates, have agreed to a ceasefire during the nationwide lockdown that has caused a slump in narcotics supply and demand — with a resultant unprecedented drop in murders.

A network of gang leaders across the country's nine provinces, known as the Council, have made funds available to members of the groups until June so they can feed their families during the shutdown, which aims to prevent the spread of the coronavirus, said Welcome Witbooi, a former gang member who mediates between gangs, local communities and the police in the Western Cape province…

Some gangs are even trying to "rebuild the relationship with the community" and are handing out food parcels to residents, he said.

Key Information: Rukshana Parker and Michael McLaggan, with photos by Halden Krog, "Cape Gangs in Lockdown: Saints or sinners in the shadow of COVID-19?" *Global Initiative Against Transnational Organized Crime*. 22 April 2020, https://globalinitiative.net/gangs-in-lockdown-manenberg/:

Two weeks into the lockdown, gangs reportedly agreed upon a 'ceasefire' to distribute food parcels to the needy. But, in some instances, food parcels are used to conceal and smuggle drugs and guns. In others, the parcels become currency to buy favour from the communities in which the gangs are active, or serve as a reward to loyal gang members and drug dealers.

Gangs are also using the COVID-19 lockdown to find new recruits and expand their territory. By providing food parcels to the desperate and the hungry, they buy loyalty. Seemingly generous acts invariably come with a price.

Key Information: Lester Kiewit, "Gangs profit though guns are silent." *Mail & Guardian*. 23 April 2020, https://mg.co.za/article/2020-04-23-gangs-profit-though-guns-are-silent/:

The illicit economy that underpins Cape Town's crime underworld has not gone into lockdown like the rest of the city or the country. But while turf wars, shootings and sporadic gang violence have been at their lowest in years, the gang economy is still operating.

A leader in the Mongrels gang in Steenberg, Cape Town, whose full name is known to the Mail & Guardian but wants to be identified only as Toufieq, said the truce is in direct response to the Covid-19 lockdown…

Policing and gang analyst Eldred De Klerk said the move by gangs to lay down the guns and concentrate on business was expected and strategic.

Gangs will not sacrifice their members to a pandemic. Manpower is their most important resource.

"Criminal gangs are engaged in conflicts on multiple fronts — amongst themselves, with law enforcement and the community. So with everyone trying to get them, you add to that coronavirus, they're like any organisation that asks 'how do we keep our members safe and how do we protect our business,'" De Klerk said.

South African National Defence Force (SANDF) and South African Police Service (SAPS) COVID-19 Checkpoint. Source: SANDF, 7 May 2020, https://twitter.com/SANDFCorpEvents/status/1258328341695864832?s=20.

Third Generation Gang Analysis

Gangs and criminal cartels—otherwise known as Criminal Armed Groups or CAGs—are responding to the COVID-19 Pandemic in a variety of ways. In some areas, CAGs exert social control where "crime groups, not police, are enforcing lockdown order in informal settlements and slums," observes Robert Muggah; in others, there is a brutal competition for dwindling drug routes leading to an escalation in violence.[2] Previous *Small Wars Journal* research notes have documented the imposition of social distancing and enforcing lockdown as well as the provision of humanitarian aid by CAGs in Brazil, El Salvador, and Mexico.[3] In these cases, a state of competitive control among the state and rival CAGs exists.[4] The lockdowns in Cape Town have led to food shortages and restrictions on the sale of alcohol and cigarettes, fueling the illicit economy and creating opportunities for corruption, gangs and organized crime.[5] Looting incidents—some believed to be sponsored by criminal organizations and gangs—have led to calls for escorts of food shipments.[6] The intense gang crime situation in Cape Town and its neighboring townships prior to the COVID-19 Pandemic led to increased police attention and the imposition of military support to police operations, setting the stage for the recent situation.[7]

Gangs in Cape Town and the Western Cape are also adapting to the challenges posed by COVID-19 and state–imposed lockdowns by enacting a truce and providing humanitarian aid to the communities where they operate. Gangs participating in the Cape Town truce reportedly include the Clever Kids, Americans, and Jesters. Social workers are hoping to expand the truce for humanitarian activities to include Hard Livings.[8]

"Americans" gangsters, Cape Town

Source: African News Agency/ANA [Used Under License]

As Parker and McLaggan of the Global Initiative Against Transnational Organized Crime have observed, the long-term effects of humanitarian intervention by the gangs is likely negligible:

> Having had time to regroup, recruit and expand their reach in communities, there is a strong likelihood that bloody turf wars between gangs will flare up again once the COVID-19 lockdown begins to ease, and police and soldiers are redeployed elsewhere.[9]

The challenges presented by pandemics to informal communities and slums are clearly evident in Cape Town. Criminal collusion in resource provision (including water and food) is blended with insecurity that, in turn, is compounded by distrust of police and informal justice provision by CAGs. The police and military may be viewed as corrupt and predatory, leading to decreased perceived legitimacy and thus opportunities for the provision of humanitarian and social goods by CAGs.[10]

Chief of Joint Operations, South African National Defence Force (SANDF) Inspecting COVID-19 Response Operations. Source: SANDF, 7 May 2020, https://twitter.com/SANDFCorpEvents/status/1258492546877095936?s=20.

This situation presents potential long-term risks in addition to short-term volatility. On the surface, lockdowns enhance fear and lead to questioning of governmental authority and legitimacy. When CAGs enter and provide social and humanitarian goods, that legitimacy is potentially further eroded. If state (police, military, and judicial) public health and law enforcement actions (collectively, police powers) are suspect, public health measures may be ignored, potentially leading to greater morbidity and mortality and conflict between the populace, gangs, and state actors. Anger and resentment mount within communities and potential arrogance and impunity on the part of public officials is a possible political liability.[11] Balancing civil rights, public health, and community safety is a necessary ingredient to negotiating the challenges posed by the pandemic which is now witnessing political and social action by CAGs (gangs and criminal enterprises).

Sources

Andrew Harding, Karen Schoonbee, and BarnebyMitchell, "How coronavirus inspired a gangland truce in South Africa." *BBC News*. 8 April 2020, https://www.bbc.com/news/av/world-africa-52205158/how-coronavirus-inspired-a-gangland-truce-in-south-africa.

Lester Kiewit, "Gangs profit though guns are silent." *Mail & Guardian*. 23 April 2020, https://mg.co.za/article/2020-04-23-gangs-profit-though-guns-are-silent/.

Rukshana Parker and Michael McLaggan, with photos by Halden Krog, "Cape Gangs in Lockdown: Saints or sinners in the shadow of COVID-19?" *Global Initiative Against Transnational Organized Crime*. 22 April 2020, https://globalinitiative.net/gangs-in-lockdown-manenberg/.

"'Literally a miracle': Violent rival gangs in South Africa call truce to help people during pandemic." *CBS News*. 18 April 2020, https://www.cbsnews.com/news/coronavirus-cape-town-violent-rival-gangs-south-africa-call-truce-pandemic/.

Loki Prinsloo and Pauline Bax, "How lockdown got gangs to declare truce amid dwindling drug sales." *Business Day*. 20 April 2020, https://www.businesslive.co.za/bd/national/2020-04-20-how-lockdown-got-gangs-to-declare-truce-amid-dwindling-drug-sales/.

Shifan Ryklief, "WATCH: Gangs in Manenberg call truce to help community weather lockdown." *Independent On Line (IOL)*. 11 April 2020, https://www.iol.co.za/news/south-africa/western-cape/watch-gangs-in-manenberg-call-truce-to-help-community-weather-lockdown-46589588.

Peta Thornycroft, "Unprecedented truce in notorious South African slums as gangs join forces to hand out coronavirus aid." *The Telegraph*. 12 April 2020, https://www.telegraph.co.uk/news/2020/04/12/unprecedented-truce-notorious-south-african-slums-gangs-join/

Tim Wyatt, "Coronavirus: Gang kingpins in South Africa call truce to help community during pandemic." *The Independent*. 20 April 2020, https://www.independent.co.uk/news/world/africa/south-africa-coronavirus-lockdown-gangs-cape-town-a9474101.html.

Endnotes

[1] Shifan Ryklief, "WATCH: Gangs in Manenberg call truce to help community weather lockdown." *Independent On Line (IOL)*. 11 April 2020, https://www.iol.co.za/news/south-africa/western-cape/watch-gangs-in-manenberg-call-truce-to-help-community-weather-lockdown-46589588.

[2] Robert Muggah, "The Pandemic Has Triggered Dramatic Shifts in the Global Criminal Underworld." *Foreign Policy*. 8 May 2020, https://foreignpolicy.com/2020/05/08/coronavirus-drug-cartels-violence-smuggling/.

[3] See John P. Sullivan, José de Arimatéia da Cruz, and Robert J. Bunker, "Third Generation Gangs Strategic Note No. 22: Rio's Gangs Impose Curfews in Response to Coronavirus." *Small Wars Journal*. 10

April 2020, https://smallwarsjournal.com/jrnl/art/third-generation-gangs-strategic-note-no-22-rios-gangs-impose-curfews-response-coronavirus; John P. Sullivan, Robert J. Bunker, and Juan Ricardo Gómez Hecht, "Third Generation Gangs Strategic Note No. 23: El Salvadoran Gangs (Maras) Enforce Domestic Quarantine / Stay at Home Orders (Cuarentena domiciliar)." *Small Wars Journal.* 5 May 2020, https://smallwarsjournal.com/jrnl/art/third-generation-gangs-strategic-note-no-23-el-salvadoran-gangs-maras-enforce-domestic; and Robert J. Bunker and John P. Sullivan, "Mexican Cartel Strategic Note No. 29: An Overview of Cartel Activities Related to COVID-19 Humanitarian Response." *Small Wars Journal.* 8 May 2020, https://smallwarsjournal.com/jrnl/art/mexican-cartel-strategic-note-no-29-overview-cartel-activities-related-covid-19.

[4] In Brazil, for example, some drug trafficking gangs (*gangues*) are imposing COVID-19 restrictions while rival militias (*milícias*) are urging a return to work leading to tensions and potential violence. See Roudabeh Kishi, "CDT Spotlight National & Local Tensions in Brazil." *CDT Spotlight*, Armed Conflict Location & Event Data Project (ACLED) COVID-19 Disorder Tracker, 12-18 April 2020, https://acleddata.com/2020/04/23/cdt-spotlight-national-local-tensions-in-brazil/.

[5] See Lynsey Chutel, "Taking on Covid-19, South Africa Goes After Cigarettes and Booze, Too." *New York Times.* 8 May 2020, https://www.nytimes.com/2020/05/08/world/africa/coronavirus-south-africa-tobacco-alcohol-ban.html and Chiara Giordano, "Coronavirus: Police caught selling black market alcohol after total ban on sale in South Africa." *The Independent.* 12 April 2020, https://www.independent.co.uk/news/world/africa/coronavirus-south-africa-alcohol-ban-lockdown-police-arrest-a9461666.html.

[6] Dan Meyer, "Food trucks to be supported by security details as looting incidents surge." *The South African.* 23 April 2020, https://www.thesouthafrican.com/news/food-trucks-looting-security-city-of-cape-town-2020/.

[7] See John P. Sullivan, "Gangs, Criminal Empires and Military Intervention in Cape Town's Crime Wars." *Small Wars Journal.* 2 February 2020, https://smallwarsjournal.com/jrnl/art/gangs-criminal-empires-and-military-intervention-cape-towns-crime-wars.

[8] Shifan Ryklief, ibid, note 1. For imagery of commodities being distributed by the gangs to local residents see the 3:07 minute video broadcast "Coronavirus Pandemic Inspires Gang Truce In South Africa." *Gist Nigeria*. #ChannelsTv #BBC #GistNigeria. 15 April 2020, https://www.youtube.com/watch?v=56EfmJNl8aI.

[9] Rukshana Parker and Michael McLaggan, with photos by Halden Krog, "Cape Gangs in Lockdown: Saints or sinners in the shadow of COVID-19?" *Global Initiative Against Transnational Organized Crime.* 22 April 2020, https://globalinitiative.net/gangs-in-lockdown-manenberg/.

[10] See Vanda Felbab-Brown and Paul Wise, "When pandemics come to slums." *Brookings.* 6 April 2020, https://www.brookings.edu/blog/order-from-chaos/2020/04/06/when-pandemics-come-to-slums/.

[11] See, for example, Stephen Grootes, "Political risks of Covid-19 lockdown, fuelled by hunger." *Daily Maverick.* 10 May 2020, https://www.dailymaverick.co.za/article/2020-05-10-political-risks-of-covid-19-lockdown-fuelled-by-hunger/.

For Additional Reading

General

John P. Sullivan, "Gangs, Criminal Empires and Military Intervention in Cape Town's Crime Wars." *Small Wars Journal*, 2 February 2020.

John P. Sullivan and Robert J. Bunker, Eds. *Strategic Notes on Third Generation Gangs*. A Small Wars Journal-El Centro Anthology. Bloomington: Xlibris, 2020.

COVID-19 Specific

John P. Sullivan, José de Arimatéia da Cruz and Robert J. Bunker, "Third Generation Gangs Strategic Note No. 22: Rio's Gangs Impose Curfews in Response to Coronavirus." *Small Wars Journal*, 10 April 2020.

John P. Sullivan, Robert J. Bunker, and Juan Ricardo Gómez Hecht, "Third Generation Gangs Strategic Note No. 23: El Salvadoran Gangs (Maras) Enforce Domestic Quarantine / Stay at Home Orders (Cuarentena domiciliar)." *Small Wars Journal*, 5 May 2020.

Robert J. Bunker and John P. Sullivan, "Mexican Cartel Strategic Note No. 29: An Overview of Cartel Activities Related to COVID-19 Humanitarian Response." *Small Wars Journal*, 8 May 2020.

Chapter 5:

Third Generation Gangs Strategic Note No. 26: COVID-19, Revolutionaries and BACRIM in Colombia

Alexandra Phelan, John P. Sullivan and Robert J. Bunker

First Published in Small Wars Journal on 2 June 2020

The COVID-19 pandemic has created opportunities and challenges for Criminal Armed Groups (CAGs)—criminal cartels, gangs, *maras*, and mafias—worldwide. This strategic note assesses the situation among Colombia's revolutionaries (the FARC – *Fuerzas Armadas Revolucionarias de Colombia*, ELN – *Ejército de Liberación Nacional*, and dissident factions, and BACRIM – *bandas criminales*. Of increasing concern is the active strategic repositioning of these entities to maximize their trans- and post-pandemic postures to the detriment of the communities within which they are embedded and the public institutions meant to represent them.

ELN Combatant. Guerrilha ELN - Colômbia Profunda 06, Source: Flickr, https://flic.kr/p/PBrf1B (CC BY-NC-SA 2.0)

Key Information: Emily Hart, "'Comply or die': Colombia's guerrillas impose their own Covid-19 lockdowns." *The Telegraph.* 23 May 2020, https://www.telegraph.co.uk/news/2020/05/23/comply-die-colombias-guerrillas-impose-covid-19-lockdowns/:

> Families are being shot dead for breaking coronavirus restrictions in rural Colombia as guerrillas enforce a brutal parallel lockdown.
>
> Armed groups, many of them dissidents of the now disbanded Farc militia, are declaring those who break the rules to be military targets in a bid to sow fear and expand their territories while the government turns a blind eye.
>
> "They are trying to reap terror and gain territorial control so that - after this crisis - people in these areas will not report them for drug trafficking, illegal mining, and corruption - the activities they carried out before and will carry out again after coronavirus…"

Key Information: "Grupos armados se expanden durante la emergencia por coronavirus en Colombia." *El Universo*. 18 May 2020, https://www.eluniverso.com/noticias/2020/05/18/nota/7844970/grupos-armados-se-expanden-durante-emergencia-coronavirus-colombia:

> En medio de la pandemia de coronavirus los grupos armados ilegales de Colombia han aprovechado las condiciones de aislamiento en el país para fortalecer su "legitimidad social", aumentar su control territorial y emprender acciones que les confieran ventaja militar, denunció este lunes la Defensoría del Pueblo.
>
> El organismo emitió una alerta temprana según la cual estos grupos ponen en riesgo a la población civil al decretar normas de conducta a partir de la regulación a establecimientos comerciales y de ocio, y del control de precios sobre víveres y materiales de sanidad.
>
> Además, bloquean las vías terrestres y fluviales de algunos lugares, y restringen la llegada de alimentos y suministros médicos.
>
> **Durante la cuarentena que comenzó el 25 de marzo la entidad ha documentado 10 homicidios en los departamentos de Arauca, Cauca y Nariño que presuntamente fueron cometidos porque las víctimas habían violado las medidas impuestas bajo amenazas, y dos de ellos fueron producto de un ataque a una misión médica.**

Key Information: "Temor el las regions del país por fin del cese al fuego del ELN." *El Tiempo*. 2 May 2020, https://www.eltiempo.com/colombia/otras-ciudades/fin-del-cese-del-fuego-del-eln-en-colombia-490880:

> Después de varias peticiones de líderes sociales y políticos para extender el cese al fuego, el Eln decidió reanudar operaciones militares este viernes primero de mayo y señaló que la pausa se **"cumplió de acuerdo a lo prometido"**.
>
> El grupo guerrillero calificó como "desafortunado que el gobierno de Iván Duque no hubiese respondido de manera recíproca ni escuchado las propuestas para avanzar en la búsqueda de la paz".

Esta situación avivó la preocupación en los habitantes de los 11 municipios que hacen parte del Catatumbo y temen el regreso de las dinámicas de guerra del Eln y que ponga en riesgo la vida de las familias campesinas.

Key Information: "¿Cómo combaten el ELN y las FARC el coronavirus?" *Semana.* 30 April 2020, https://www.semana.com/nacion/articulo/como-combaten-el-eln-y-las-farc-el-coronavirus/667376:

El Ejército de Liberación Nacional, ELN, aseguró que la llegada del coronavirus los tomó por sorpresa, igual que al Gobierno y que su ideal en este momento es que el contagio no llegue a las zonas de influencia del país donde ellos tienen presencia.

"De la mano con las medidas de confinamiento que se han tomado, también en las zonas se ha promovido evitar el flujo de pasajeros y tomar medidas para la carga y el transporte de mercancía y de comida sobre todo, para evitar que llegue el virus a nuestras zonas", aseguró alias 'Uriel' uno de los comandantes más buscados por las Fuerzas Militares.

En diálogo con SEMANA, 'Uriel' dijo que ante la pandemia, el ELN pretende estar más retirado de la población y centrar sus esfuerzos en entrenar mejor a su gente y afianzar los procesos de formación mediante el desarrollo de escuelas.

"Está más parado ese proceso que llamamos 'Trabajo político administrative', que es el trabajo de acompañamiento a las comunidades." Asimismo, aseguró que aún no se han registrado personas con el cuadro patológico del covid-19 y que se está evitando a toda costa que entren personas externas a las comunidades para prolongar la probabilidad de contagio que puede haber.

Key Information: "¿Grupos criminales aprovechan pandemia para fortalecer sus negocios ilícitos?" *VerdadAbierta.com.* 8 April 2020, https://verdadabierta.com/grupos-criminales-aprovechan-pandemia-para-fortalecer-sus-negocios-ilicitos/:

En zonas de Antioquia, Cauca, Córdoba y Nariño han circulado mensajes de organizaciones armadas en los que hacen llamados perentorios a los pobladores para que se tomen en serio la cuarentena decretada desde el 23 marzo. Además, la presión a las comunidades también es por temor a contagiarse y morir, o caer presos al buscar asistencia médica.

Sobre el tema son pocas las autoridades que hablan, y aquellas que se atreven a hacerlo dicen desconocer del tema, además de que solicitan no ser identificados por razones de seguridad. Quienes sí hablan, a cambio de mantener su anonimato, son algunos líderes sociales y analistas regionales. Unos y otros expresan sus preocupaciones por el impacto que las supuestas imposiciones de presuntos grupos armados ilegales tienen entre unas comunidades atemorizadas por el creciente número de infectados por Covid-19 en el país y su empobrecimiento debido al aislamiento al que están sometidas.

Este portal se dio a la tarea de recopilar mensajes emitidos al parecer por distintas organizaciones armadas ilegales. Se obtuvieron panfletos, mensajes en redes sociales y fotografías a nombre de las Guerrillas Unidas del Pacífico (Gup); el Frente Oliver Sinisterra; las Autodefensas Gaitanistas de Colombia (Agc); disidencias del Frente 18 de las Farc; el Bloque Virgilio Peralta Arenas; disidencias del Frente 6 de las Farc; y la guerrilla del Eln.

Key Information: Carlos Cerón, "En medio de controles por Covid-19 disidencias de Farc pintan vehículos en Cauca." W Radio. 25 March 2020, https://www.wradio.com.co/noticias/regionales/en-medio-de-controles-por-covid19-disidencias-de-farc-pintan-vehiculos-en-cauca/20200325/nota/4025700.aspx:

> Presuntos integrantes de la estructura Dagoberto Ramos, disidencia de las Farc, aprovecharon los controles que se realizan para evitar la propagación del coronavirus y **pintaron grafitis en algunos vehículos en zona rural del norte del Cauca…**
>
> Entre tanto, se informó que, entre los sectores de La Chivera y Pajarito del municipio de Caloto, y en otros sitios como Río Negro y San Francisco, Toribío y en la vereda El Filo, entre Balboa y Argelia, **se registraron retenes ilegales por parte de sujetos armados.**
>
> Organismos judiciales investigan versiones que indican que los individuos aprovecharon los controles que las autoridades indígenas y civiles de esas zonas realizan para evitar la propagación del coronavirus, y ejecutaron este tipo de acciones.

En el municipio de Argelia **también fue advertida la presencia de disidencias de las Farc, estructura Carlos Patiño.**

Key Information: "Con amenazas, disidencia de las Farc dice que hará cumplir cuarentena en Nariño." *Tubarco*. 25 March 2020, https://tubarco.news/tubarco-noticias-occidente/tubarco-noticias-narino-tubarco-noticias-occidente/con-amenazas-disidencia-de-las-farc-dice-que-hara-cumplir-cuarentena-en-narino/:

> La disidencia 29 con injerencia en Nariño recalcó que declarará como objetivo militar a quien infrinja las medidas contra el coronavirus.
>
> Preocupada dijo sentirse la disidencia del frente 29 de las antiguas Farc en Nariño por la desobediencia ante las medidas restrictivas para evitar la propagación del coronavirus.
>
> A través de un panfleto manifestó que hará cumplir el aislamiento obligatorio en municipios de la cordillera de Nariño y sur del Cauca.
>
> "Persona que sea observada en la calle en diversas ocasiones será multada y si reiteran serán objetivo militar", precisa la disidencia…
>
> La disidencia del frente 29 de las Farc Estiven González libra una fuerte disputa territorial contra bandas criminales y el propio Eln…

Third Generation Gang Analysis

The COVID-19 pandemic has exposed the seams in the varied relationships between the state and organized crime.[1] In Latin America, criminal armed groups (CAGs) including Mexican cartels, Brazilian prison-street gang complexes, along with *maras* in El Salvador (and throughout the Northern Triangle of Central America – NTCA) have exploited the situation to further their goals.[2] Similar situations have been seen among mafias in Italy and gangs in South Africa.[3]

COVID-19 has also presented opportunities and challenges to CAGs in Colombia. In some cases, CAGs and insurgents have leveraged the crisis in order to further expand proto-authority while simultaneously aiming to enhance and consolidate social legitimacy. FARC dissidents have managed to double their membership over a one-year period (since May 2019), going from roughly 2,600 members to almost 4,600 and present in 138 municipalities. It is alleged that 2,600 are armed combatants while another 2,000 belong to clandestine support networks.[4] The largest fronts are led by "Gentil Duarte," and former FARC leaders "Iván Márquez" and "Jesús Santrich," and have established structures in Guaviare, Vaupés, Meta, Arauca, Guainía, Vichada, and Casanar.

Soon after a nationwide quarantine was decreed on 24 March, CAGs throughout the country began to enforce lockdown measures in areas of territorial influence and control. Colombian news outlet *VerdadAbierta*[5] compiled pamphlets, messages on social media, and photographs where such communiqués warned communities that they must comply with the mandatory preventive isolation decreed by the Colombian government. These communiques were obtained from the United Guerrillas of the Pacific (*Guerrillas Unidas del Pacífico* – GUP), the Oliver Sinisterra Front, the Gulf Clan (*Clan del Golfo*, or Self-Defense Forces of Colombia/*Guerrillas Unidas del Pacífico* – AGC), FARC dissidents' 18 and 6 Fronts, the Virgilio Peralta Arenas Block, and the ELN. These messages were obtained throughout the departments of Cauca, Antioquia, Córdoba, and Nariño.

Colombia's Ombudsman's Office issued an early warning that CAGs were taking advantage of the isolation period in order to expand territorial control and use the pandemic to their military advantage.[6] Specifically, civilian populations under areas of CAG influence are at heightened risk where there is not only the fear of catching or dying from COVID-19 and economic and social vulnerabilities, but also illegal armed groups that are, in many respects, arbitrarily imposing control orders in various regions throughout Colombia. For example, the Ombudsman's Office warned that CAGs were regulating commercial and leisure establishments, controlling food and medical supply prices, blocking land and waterways in some regions, and restricting the arrival of food and medicine. Concerningly, the Office documented at least ten homicides in the Arauca, Cauca, and Nariño departments that were allegedly committed because the victims had violated measures imposed by CAGs.[7] Two homicides were alleged to be the result of an attack on a medical mission in Nariño.[8]

Responding to COVID-19, the ELN ordered a month-long ceasefire from 1 April until 30 April as a "humanitarian gesture" towards the Colombian population "suffering from the devastation of coronavirus."[9] They argued that the ceasefire was "active," insofar that they reserved the right to "defend themselves" against the attacks carried out by state forces, paramilitaries, and drug trafficking organisations throughout various regions of the country. The ELN also called on President Duque of Colombia to meet with the ELN's delegation in Havana to discuss a temporary, bilateral ceasefire, using the crisis as an opportunity to resume peace talks. In a *Semana* interview with commander "Uriel" of ELN's Western Bloc, it was noted that the ELN intended to withdraw from popular mobilisation to focus on "Administrative Political Work," which included shifting efforts to training their combatants and develop schools to "strengthen training processes."[10] The ceasefire ended on 1 May, with ELN leaders claiming [that the Duque administration was not interested in negotiations yet the ELN allege that they had "no offensive plans" during the crisis.[11]

Organized criminal enterprises—including the range of CAGs—are resilient entities. They are formed by a variety of networks spanning local and global licit, mixed, and illicit political economies. CAGs, like other organized crime groups, are adaptive and resilient, constantly reinforcing their power and potentials for profit.[12] They can be inhibited by interruptions of global illicit flows but will reinforce their organizational capacity by seeking new opportunities for territorial control, governance, and profit.[13] Yet, these opportunities are not all positive expressions of humanitarian concern and 'social banditry' as described in numerous cases.[14] In some cases, these opportunities are occasions for renewed or accelerated armed violence as CAGs seek relative superiority over their rivals and the state for territorial control and economic dominance.[15] Moreover, the arbitrary enforcement of self-imposed laws by CAGs raise grave concerns for civilian populations already living in vulnerable regions, coupled with new risks posed by the pandemic.

National Liberation Army/*Ejército de Liberación Nacional* (ELN)
COVID-19 Quarantine (*Cuarentena*) Notice [16]
Source: @jmantillaba, Twitter. 26 March 2020,
https://twitter.com/jmantillaba/status/1243155042812727296/photo/2.

Sources

Carlos Cerón, "En medio de controles por Covid-19 disidencias de Farc pintan vehículos en Cauca." W Radio. 25 March 2020, https://www.wradio.com.co/noticias/regionales/en-medio-de-controles-por-covid19-disidencias-de-farc-pintan-vehiculos-en-cauca/20200325/nota/4025700.aspx.

"¿Cómo combaten el ELN y las FARC el coronavirus?" *Semana*. 30 April 2020, https://www.semana.com/nacion/articulo/como-combaten-el-eln-y-las-farc-el-coronavirus/667376.

"Con amenazas, disidencia de las Farc dice que hará cumplir cuarentena en Nariño." *Tubarco*. 25 March 2020, https://tubarco.news/tubarco-noticias-occidente/tubarco-noticias-narino-tubarco-noticias-occidente/con-amenazas-disidencia-de-las-farc-dice-que-hara-cumplir-cuarentena-en-narino/.

"Grupos armados se expanden durante la emergencia por coronavirus en Colombia." *El Universo*. 18 May 2020, https://www.eluniverso.com/noticias/2020/05/18/nota/7844970/grupos-armados-se-expanden-durante-emergencia-coronavirus-colombia.

"¿Grupos criminales aprovechan pandemia para fortalecer sus negocios ilícitos?" *VerdadAbierta.com*. April 2020, https://verdadabierta.com/grupos-criminales-aprovechan-pandemia-para-fortalecer-sus-negocios-ilicitos/.

Emily Hart, "'Comply or die': Colombia's guerrillas impose their own Covid-19 lockdowns." *The Telegraph*. 23 May 2020, https://www.telegraph.co.uk/news/2020/05/23/comply-die-colombias-guerrillas-impose-covid-19-lockdowns/.

"Temor el las regions del país por fin del cese al fuego del ELN." *El Tiempo*. 2 May 2020, https://www.eltiempo.com/colombia/otras-ciudades/fin-del-cese-del-fuego-del-eln-en-colombia-490880.

Endnotes

{1} See, for example, Whitney Eulich and Ana Ionova, "A helping hand? Amid pandemic, gangs cast themselves as protectors." *Christian Science Monitor*. 19 May 2020, https://www.csmonitor.com/World/Americas/2020/0519/A-helping-hand-Amid-pandemic-gangs-cast-themselves-as-protectors.

[2] This is the fourth strategic note in a series covering CAGs and COVID-19 in Latin America, including Mexico). See John P. Sullivan, José de Arimatéia da Cruz and Robert J. Bunker, "Third Generation Gangs Strategic Note No. 22: Rio's Gangs Impose Curfews in Response to Coronavirus." *Small Wars Journal*. 10 April 2020, https://smallwarsjournal.com/jrnl/art/third-generation-gangs-strategic-note-no-22-rios-gangs-impose-curfews-response-coronavirus; John P. Sullivan, Robert J. Bunker and Juan Ricardo Gómez Hecht, "Third Generation Gangs Strategic Note No. 23: El Salvadoran Gangs (Maras) Enforce Domestic Quarantine / Stay at Home Orders (Cuarentena domiciliar)." *Small Wars Journal*. 5 May 2020, https://smallwarsjournal.com/jrnl/art/third-generation-gangs-strategic-note-no-23-el-salvadoran-gangs-maras-enforce-domestic; and Robert J. Bunker and John P. Sullivan, "Mexican Cartel Strategic Note No. 29: An Overview of Cartel Activities Related to COVID-19 Humanitarian Response." *Small Wars Journal*. 8 May 2020, https://smallwarsjournal.com/jrnl/art/mexican-cartel-strategic-note-no-29-overview-cartel-activities-related-covid-19.

[3] On COVID-19 and the Italian mafias, see Anna Sergi, "Organised crime and COVID-19." *Essex Social Science on COVID-19*. 20 May 2020 Webinar by @Uni_of_Essex on Vimeo, https://vimeo.com/421004597 and Luchiano Pollchieni, "Rule, support and buy: Making sense of Mafia strategies in the COVID-19 aftermath." Urban Violence Research Network (UVRN). 18 May 2020, https://urbanviolence.org/rule-support-and-buy/. On COVID-19 and gangs in South Africa, see John P. Sullivan and Robert J. Bunker, "Third Generation Gangs Strategic Note No. 24: COVID-19, Gangs and Lockdown in Cape Town." *Small Wars Journal*. 18 May 2020, https://smallwarsjournal.com/jrnl/art/third-generation-gangs-strategic-note-no-24-covid-19-gangs-and-lockdown-cape-town. Japan's Yakuza has also been reported to seek advantage from the coronavirus pandemic. See Alessia Cerantola, "Japanese Gangs Vie for Power Amid Pandemic." *OCCRP: Organized Crime and Corruption Reporting Project*. 22 April 2020, https://www.occrp.org/en/coronavirus/japanese-gangs-vie-for-power-amid-pandemic.

[4] See "Disidencias de las FARC duplican su número de hombres en solo 12 meses." *El Tiempo*. 31 May 2020, https://www.eltiempo.com/unidad-investigativa/disidencias-de-las-farc-duplican-su-numero-de-hombres-en-armas-solo-12-meses-501426.

[5] See "¿Grupos criminales aprovechan pandemia para fortalecer sus negocios ilícitos?" *VerdadAbierta.com*. 8 April 2020, https://verdadabierta.com/grupos-criminales-aprovechan-pandemia-para-fortalecer-sus-negocios-ilicitos/.

[6] See "Grupos armados se expanden durante la emergencia por coronavirus en Colombia." *El Universo*. 18 May 2020, https://www.eluniverso.com/noticias/2020/05/18/nota/7844970/grupos-armados-se-expanden-durante-emergencia-coronavirus-colombia.

[7] Ibid.

[8] See "Ataque a misión médica en Nariño deja dos personas Muertos." RNC Radio. 4 April 2020, https://www.rcnradio.com/colombia/sur/ataque-mision-medica-en-narino-deja-dos-personas-muertas.

[9] See "El ELN Frente A La Pandemia Por El Coronavirus COVID-19." *ELN Voces*. 30 March 2020, https://eln-voces.net/el-eln-frente-a-la-pandemia-por-el-coronavirus-covid-19/.

[10] See "¿Cómo combaten el ELN y las FARC el coronavirus?" *Semana*. 30 April 2020, https://www.semana.com/nacion/articulo/como-combaten-el-eln-y-las-farc-el-coronavirus/667376.

[11] "Colombia's ELN rebels have 'no offensive plans' during coronavirus crisis." *Colombia Reports*. 4 May 2020, https://colombiareports.com/colombias-eln-rebels-have-no-offensive-plans-but-defensive-plans-during-coronavirus-crisis/.

[12] Fabian Zhila, "The Leviathan of Organised Crime." *RUSI – Strategic Hub on Organised Crime*. 21 May 2020, https://shoc.rusi.org/informer/leviathon-organised-crime.

[13] See Benoit Gomis, "How the Illicit Drug Trade Is Adapting to the Coronavirus Pandemic." *World Politics Review*. 20 April 2020, https://www.worldpoliticsreview.com/articles/28696/how-the-illicit-drug-trade-is-adapting-to-the-coronavirus-pandemic.

[14] See, for example, the cases described in Notes 1 and 2. For background, see John P. Sullivan, "Criminal Insurgency: Narcocultura, Social Banditry, and Information Operations." *Small Wars Journal*. 3 December 2012, https://smallwarsjournal.com/jrnl/art/criminal-insurgency-narcocultura-social-banditry-and-information-operations.

[15] While all three type of CAGs discussed in this strategic note (FARC, ELN, and BACRIM) have leveraged the COVID-19 situation for political and territorial advantage, the threat of armed violence remains. See "Broken Ties, Frozen Borders: Colombia and Venezuela Face COVID-19." *Crisis Group Latin America Briefing N°42*. Bogotá/Brussels: International Crisis Group. 15 April 2020, https://www.crisisgroup.org/latin-america-caribbean/andes/colombia/b24-broken-ties-frozen-borders-colombia-and-venezuela-face-covid-19.

[16] For a COVID-19 quarantine (*cuarentena*) notice distributed by the Frente Oliver Sinisterra FARC-EP on 20 March 2020, see @jmantillaba, Twitter. 26 March 2020, https://twitter.com/jmantillaba/status/1243155042812727296/photo/1.

For Additional Reading

Alexandra Phelan, Nuri Veronika, Helem Stenger and Irine Gayatri, "COVID-19 and violent extremist groups: adapting to an evolving crisis." *Monash Lens*, 28 April 2020.

John P. Sullivan, José de Arimatéia da Cruz and Robert J. Bunker, "Third Generation Gangs Strategic Note No. 22: Rio's Gangs Impose Curfews in Response to Coronavirus." *Small Wars Journal*, 10 April 2020.

John P. Sullivan, Robert J. Bunker and Juan Ricardo Gómez Hecht, "Third Generation Gangs Strategic Note No. 23: El Salvadoran Gangs (Maras) Enforce Domestic Quarantine / Stay at Home Orders (Cuarentena domiciliar)." *Small Wars Journal*, 5 May 2020.

Robert J. Bunker and John P. Sullivan, "Mexican Cartel Strategic Note No. 29: An Overview of Cartel Activities Related to COVID-19 Humanitarian Response." *Small Wars Journal*, 8 May 2020.

John P. Sullivan and Robert Bunker, "Third Generation Gangs Strategic Note No. 24: COVID-19, Gangs and Lockdown in Cape Town." *Small Wars Journal*, 18 May 2020.

John P. Sullivan and Robert J. Bunker, Eds., *Strategic Notes on Third Generation Gangs*. A Small Wars Journal-El Centro Anthology. Bloomington: Xlibris, 2020.

Chapter 6

Third Generation Gangs Strategic Note No. 27: COVID-19 and Transnational Italian Mafias

Anna Sergi, John P. Sullivan and Robert J. Bunker

First Published in Small Wars Journal on 2 June 2020

The COVID-19 pandemic has created opportunities and challenges for transnational organized crime groups, and mafias worldwide. This strategic note assesses the situation among the Italian mafias, including the Sicilian mafia, camorra, and 'ndragheta. The widening vacuum of state governance along with the collapse of the financial system is concerning as it has resulted in organized criminal entities increasingly usurping the provision of public goods and services and undermining legitimate sectors of the formal economy such as the banking services and health care.

Carabinieri COVID-19 control activities to protect the public health and counter illicit trade in personal protective masks. Source: Il Viminale (Italian Ministry of the Interior, @Viminale). Twitter, 29 May 2020, https://twitter.com/Viminale/status/1261971332302061569?s=20.

Key Information: Jamie Dettmer, "As Crime Dips Worldwide, Agile Syndicates Adapt to Pandemic." Voice of America. 29 January 2020, https://www.voanews.com/covid-19-pandemic/crime-dips-worldwide-agile-syndicates-adapt-pandemic:

> Organized crime groups have been taking advantage of fresh opportunities presented by the pandemic, from acting surreptitiously as suppliers to governments, to serving as "partners of the state in maintaining order," warns a recent report by the Global Initiative Against Transnational Organized Crime, a network of independent global and regional experts headquartered in Geneva, Switzerland…
>
> …In Italy, mafia groups have taken advantage of rising poverty and economic desperation in the south to present themselves as an alternative to the state…
>
> …Investigative journalist Roberto Saviano, author of *Gomorra*, a bestseller on the Naples-based Camorra mafia, told *la Repubblica* newspaper, "The pandemic is the ideal place for mafias, and the reason is simple — if you are hungry, you are looking for bread; it does not matter which oven it is baked from and who it is distributing it."

Key Information: Daniela De Lorenzo, "Italy: Camorra mafia clan attempts comeback amid coronavirus." *Deutsche Welle*. 24 May 2020, https://www.dw.com/en/italy-camorra-mafia-clan-attempts-comeback-amid-coronavirus/a-53532200:

> Plagued by COVID-19 and an economic crisis, Italy is now facing the possible resurgence of the Camorra clan. The crime syndicate, like others across Italy, is trying to exploit the post-lockdown vacuum…

> …Plagued by COVID-19 and an economic crisis, Italy is now facing the possible resurgence of the Camorra clan. The crime syndicate, like others across Italy, is trying to exploit the post-lockdown vacuum…

Key Information: Melissa Barra, "Faced with the Covid-19 crisis, the Italian mafia sees business opportunities." France 24. 2 May 2020, https://www.france24.com/en/20200502-faced-with-the-covid-19-crisis-the-italian-mafia-sees-business-opportunities:

> **Italy's mafia has worked out how to profit from the coronavirus pandemic and the resulting economic crash. From offering opportunistic social aid and usurious loans to new business investments, the mafia is all set to exploit the vulnerable…**

> …Faced with a dramatic increase in people on the poverty line, the Italian government announced the distribution of €400 million in shopping vouchers. The Italian agricultural union Coldiretti reported that requests for food aid from charity organisations such as Caritas increased by 30% in March, according to AFP.

> At the same time, the authorities and several media outlets noted that mafia groups started distributing their own food baskets to families facing financial difficulties. Some considered this both a strategy of recruitment and of social consensus. It coincided, too, with a number of key mafia bosses being allowed to exchange their prison cells for house arrest, thereby returning to the territories they controlled…

> …The lockdown and the resulting economic catastrophe has put many small businesses at risk of bankruptcy. "Banks tend to lend little to SMEs (small and medium enterprises). They

must then turn to more shadowy operations and the mafia offers them fresh, albeit dirty, money," Clotilde Champeyrache, a lecturer at the University of Paris 8, a mafia specialist and author of "La Face cachée de l'économie" (The Hidden Face of the Economy) explained to FRANCE 24.

Key Information: Valentina Di Donato and Tim Lister, "The Mafia is poised to exploit coronavirus, and not just in Italy." CNN. 19 April 2020, https://www.cnn.com/2020/04/19/europe/italy-mafia-exploiting-coronavirus-crisis-aid-intl/index.html:

> Senior anti-mafia officials and researchers have told CNN that Mafia clans are already taking advantage of the coronavirus pandemic, especially in southern Italy.
>
> They are providing everyday necessities in poor neighborhoods, offering credit to businesses on the verge of bankruptcy and planning to siphon off a chunk of the billions of euros being lined up in stimulus funds.
>
> The most powerful branch of the Mafia—the 'Ndrangheta, based in Calabria—is thought to control 80% of the European cocaine market. Even as the pandemic made distribution more difficult, it took advantage of the lockdown…
>
> But Mafia groups are about far more than trafficking cocaine. They are deeply embedded in the economy.

Key Information: Anna Sergi, "Effetti indesiderati del Covid-19: sei opportunità per le mafie" [Undesirable effects of Covid-19: six opportunities for mafias]. *La Via Libera*. 19 March 2020, https://lavialibera.libera.it/it-schede-65-gli_effetti_indesiderati_del_coronavirus_le_sei_opportunita_illecite_per_le_mafie:

> *Six profiles of risk are highlighted in this article related to both mafia-type groups and other groups seeking opportunities due to Covid-19 crisis, especially the financial crisis. These six opportunities, summarized below relate to:*
>
> 1. The impact on illicit trafficking: with a specific focus on how different illicit trade will be impacted differently.

2. Drug consumptions: as above, different narcotics are impacted differently for production and transport issues.
3. Emerging markets: these could be in the health care provisions as much as in online fraud and gambling activities.
4. Loansharking and acquisition of firms: very typical in financial crisis, for mafia-type groups to use their cash to lend money to struggling businesses so that they can afterwards be taken over.
5. Corruption: occasional corruption for profit as well as public administration corruption might increase.
6. Governance and control of territory: mafia-type groups' relationships with their territories in lockdown can lend itself to tighter relationships with local actors.[1]

Key Information: Luca Rinaldi, "L'economia criminale del post-emergenza Covid-19" [Criminal economy post Covid-19 emergency]. *IrpiMedia*. 6 April 2020, https://irpimedia.irpi.eu/covid19-economia-criminale-post-virus/:

This article focuses mostly on the post-pandemic environment, highlighting how the pandemic financial crisis can create new vulnerabilities that organised crime groups in Italy can exploit.

The Adjunct Chief Prosecutor for Reggio Calabria, Giuseppe Lombardo, is quoted saying: "we will go beyond the usual scheme of loansharking in its traditional forms…" as the most vulnerable sectors, especially to the 'ndrangheta, are going to be real estate and health care in the medium and longer terms. Investments, financing, cyber-fraud and public-private collusion will be the key for criminal exploitation of the post-Covid.[2]

Key Information: Salvo Palazzolo, "Mafia, blitz fra Palermo e Milano: 91 arresti. Ex concorrente del Grande fratello prestanome dei boss" [Mafia, blitz between Palermo and Milano: 91 arrests. Former participant to the Big Brother as shadow of the bosses]. *La Repubblica*. 12 May 2020, https://palermo.repubblica.it/cronaca/2020/05/12/news/mafia_blitz_fra_palermo_e_milano-256341141/?refresh_ce:

This article reports on a large operation that brought to the arrest in both Sicily and Lombardia regions, of the historical Fontana clan. They were managing a business involved in the sale of coffee, using shadow businesses men not to raise suspicion. Although many activities the clans were involved in referred to the prior-Covid period, there was an indication that the clans were ready to step up during the pandemic.

The judge for preliminary investigations in Palermo is quoted saying how "the clans are ready to exploit the Covid emergency to take over businesses—with the crisis of liquidity that entrepreneurs and shop owners will be facing, these clans wanted to intervene by using their cash to practice loansharking and lend money at very high rates, so that they can later take over assets and companies in an extortive manner."[3]

Key Information: Redazione, "Camorra e Covid. Una fonte rivela: 'Gli usurai hanno già preso alcune attività a sud di Napoli,'" [A source reveals: "The moneylenders have already taken some activities south of Naples]. *La Via Libera*. 15 May 2020, https://lavialibera.libera.it/it-schede-128-camorra_e_covid_una_fonte_rivela_gli_usurai_hanno_gia_preso_alcune_attivita_a_sud_di_napoli:

This article reports on the insights from an informant in Naples, relating to the activities of some camorra clans in the city since lockdown. Camorra families are exploiting lockdown in two ways: on the one hand they have offered some support, food and necessary products; on the other hand they have been ready to offer cash and resources to people who want to keep their lifestyle and business intact. The informant says:

"Help to families, food and other goods, are nothing new. In the city there are areas where some deal drugs, some is a gatekeeper, some others are selling stuff, everyone keeps quiet, as everyone is involved. That has not changed with Covid. The pandemic has, however offered new opportunities, also allowing some families to cross over to near neighborhoods, to liaise with one another and offer support."[4]

Third Generation Gang Analysis

The COVID-19 pandemic has exposed the seams in the varied relationships between the state and organized crime.[5]

June 2020 issue of *Polizia Moderna* focusing on the '*Pandemia mafiosa*,'
Source: *Polizia Moderna*, Italian State Police (*Polizia di Stato*), June 2020, https://poliziamoderna.poliziadistato.it/statics/23/cover_06-20_big.jpg.

Different clans of Italian mafia-type groups throughout the whole country are affected differently by the pandemic closures and lockdown of activities. The impediment to mobility will be affected differently in the aftermath of COVID-19 emergency, when the financial crisis will boost the already vast Italian informal economy and create new opportunities for both criminal enterprises and infiltration in the legal economy. From the perspective of illicit activities, mafia groups are polycrime groups: their portfolio of activities span from extortion to money laundering, from drug trafficking to fraud in public and EU funds. Not all clans have the same capacities.[6]

Mafia groups in Italy—camorra clans in Campania and some Northern regions, 'ndrangheta clans in Calabria and in the rest of Italy, cosa nostra clans in Sicily and also in the majority of other regions—form an archipelago of these different clans doing different things concurrently. Italian authorities have warned that the main cause for concern at this stage of the COVID-19 pandemic relates to the financial crisis and the collapse of commercial activities and businesses.[7] Indeed, clans of all Italian mafia groups are able to operate loansharking schemes, whereby they are able to inject cash into struggling businesses so that afterwards they can acquire the businesses should the debt, at extortive rates, not be paid.

All Italian mafia groups have been adapting quite fast to the changing conditions imposed by the pandemic. 'Ndrangheta clans have been able to continue most of their cocaine trafficking as they have a very wide distribution network for cocaine across all Italy, which has been useful in times of mobility restrictions.[8] Additionally, different drug trafficking groups have been cooperating with each other in ways that were not usual prior to the pandemic. For example, Sicilian mafia groups of cosa nostra, have been getting more and more involved in retail distribution of drugs to avoid delays and hiccups in the drug trade.[9] Different criminal businesses have been affected differently; for example, extortion, which is an evergreen criminal activity for many 'ndrangheta, cosa nostra and camorra clans have obviously suffered the pitfalls of shops and businesses shutting down. However, as extortion takes many forms with Italian mafias (e.g., the imposition of certain products or sponsorships), this activity is expected to resurge as soon as commercial activities start running again.[10]

The COVID-19 pandemic has exacerbated economic tensions and enhanced political opportunities for mafias in Italy and similar groups worldwide.[11] Some Italian mafia groups have used the pandemic to provide humanitarian aid—such as distributing food parcels—in order to leverage their stature, enhance their perceived legitimacy in the community, and exert social suasion and territorial control. Although this is a practice not often observed during the pandemic (as only a few cases in Sicily and Campania have been reported), it confirms a typical feature of mafia groups. What differentiates mafia-type groups from other organized crime networks is, in fact, the will to power and to govern.[12] Mafia leaders view themselves as power brokers and aspire to "govern territories and markets."[13][14]

In times of lockdown, mafia clans, like everyone else, have gone back to their own neighborhoods. Depending on the connection they have with their communities, they can either provide relief and support or exploit their power to get advantages. In the former, this will produce a sense of gratitude in the population that will eventually be useful for future political and communal endorsements. In the latter, this could result in mafia members receiving privileged treatment in, for example receiving health care and assistance.[15]

Once the pandemic is over, and the lockdown measures are lifted, mafia groups' survival will also depend on the communities they are both nourishing as well as exploiting. This might lead to interesting outcomes. For example, we may see clans undertaking new types of political engagements, such as the infiltration of municipal administrations or *politica mafiosa*[16] and administrating public funds through compromised companies, defrauding the state and the EU, as recently seen in Calabria.[17] In an ironic twist, the infiltration of *mafiosi* into legitimate enterprises may also include the potential infiltration of the lucrative health care sector leading to the ability to launder money and extract profit making the situation a true '*pandemia mafiosa.*'[18]

Sources

Melissa Barra, "Faced with the Covid-19 crisis, the Italian mafia sees business opportunities." France 24. 2 May 2020, https://www.france24.com/en/20200502-faced-with-the-covid-19-crisis-the-italian-mafia-sees-business-opportunities.

Jamie Dettmer, "As Crime Dips Worldwide, Agile Syndicates Adapt to Pandemic." Voice of America. 29 January 2020, https://www.voanews.com/covid-19-pandemic/crime-dips-worldwide-agile-syndicates-adapt-pandemic.

Daniela De Lorenzo, "Italy: Camorra mafia clan attempts comeback amid coronavirus." *Deutsche Welle*. 24 May 2020, https://www.dw.com/en/italy-camorra-mafia-clan-attempts-comeback-amid-coronavirus/a-53532200.

Valentina Di Donato and Tim Lister, "The Mafia is poised to exploit coronavirus, and not just in Italy." CNN. 19 April 2020, https://www.cnn.com/2020/04/19/europe/italy-mafia-exploiting-coronavirus-crisis-aid-intl/index.html.

Sergio Nazzaro, "Pandemia mafiosa," (Mafia Pandemic], *Polizia Moderna*, June 2020, https://poliziamoderna.poliziadistato.it/articolo/3535ed118c7b4065180711109.

Salvo Palazzolo, "Mafia, blitz fra Palermo e Milano: 91 arresti. Ex concorrente del Grande fratello prestanome dei boss" [Mafia, blitz between Palermo and Milano: 91 arrests. Former participant to the Big Brother as shadow of the bosses]. *La Repubblica*. 12 May 2020, https://palermo.repubblica.it/cronaca/2020/05/12/news/mafia_blitz_fra_palermo_e_milano-256341141/?refresh_ce.

Redazione, "Camorra e Covid. Una fonte rivela: 'Gli usurai hanno già preso alcune attività a sud di Napoli,'" [A source reveals: "The moneylenders have already taken some activities south of Naples"]. *La Via Libera*. 15 May 2020, https://lavialibera.libera.it/it-schede-128-camorra_e_covid_una_fonte_rivela_gli_usurai_hanno_gia_preso_alcune_attivita_a_sud_di_napoli.

Luca Rinaldi, "L'economia criminale del post-emergenza Covid-19" [Criminal economy post Covid-19 emergency]. *IrpiMedia*. 6 April 2020 https://irpimedia.irpi.eu/covid19-economia-criminale-post-virus/.

Lorenzo Tondo, "Mafia distributes food to Italy's struggling residents." *The Guardian*. 10 April 2020, https://www.theguardian.com/world/2020/apr/10/mafia-distributes-food-to-italys-struggling-residents#maincontent.

Audrey Wilson, "Goodbye Government. Hello Mafia." *Foreign Policy.* 22 May 2020, https://foreignpolicy.com/2020/05/22/goodbye-government-hello-mafia-coronavirus-pandemic-crisis-nonstate-organized-crime-insurgency-charity-conflict/.

Endnotes

[1] In the original Italian text: 1. I traffici illeciti; 2. Il consumo di droghe; 3. Nuovi gruppi e nuovi mercati; 4. L'usura e l'acquisizione di attività; 5. La corruzione; 6. La protezione e il controllo.

[2] From the original Italian text: "Qui si andrà oltre lo schema del prestito a usura che, come ha sottolineato alcuni giorni fa sul Fatto Quotidiano il procuratore aggiunto di Reggio Calabria Giuseppe Lombardo, «continuerà a esistere solo quale reato tipico delle manifestazioni criminali meno ramificate ed evolute». Dunque la seconda fase di fatto setterà l'agenda criminale sul medio-lungo periodo toccando settori come il mercato immobiliare e la sanità arrivando a consolidare le proprie posizioni, ha sottolineato ancora Lombardo, anche all'interno del mercato creditizio e dei beni di prima necessità. Nei settori in cui arriveranno investimenti, finanziamenti a pioggia e appalti saranno necessarie regolamentazioni importanti anche per arginare i sistemi corruttivi."

[3] From the original Italian text: "l gip che ha firmato l'ordinanza di custodia cautelare, Piergiorgio Morosini, rilancia l'allarme: "I clan sono pronti ad approfittare della situazione attuale, sono sempre pronti a dare la caccia ad aziende in stato di necessità – ha scritto nel suo provvedimento - Con la crisi di liquidità di cui soffrono imprenditori e commercianti, i componenti dell'organizzazione mafiosa potrebbero intervenire dando fondo ai loro capitali illecitamente accumulati per praticare l'usura e per poi rilevare beni e aziende con manovre estorsive, in tal modo ulteriormente alterando la libera concorrenza."

[4] From the original Italian text: "Gli aiuti alle famiglie, alimentari e di altro genere, non sono una novità. Nel comune c'è una grossa piazza di spaccio e lì, tra gli abitanti del quartiere, c'è chi fa la vedetta, chi custodisce, chi smista, chi vende, insomma sono quasi tutti coinvolti e il silenzio viene pagato, adesso come prima di Covid. La pandemia ha però fornito nuove opportunità, permettendo a certe famiglie di sconfinare dalle zone in cui operano solitamente, per rivolgersi ad altri quartieri e persino ai comuni limitrofi."

[5] This is the sixth strategic note in a series covering criminal enterprises and COVID-19 See See John P. Sullivan, José de Arimatéia da Cruz, and Robert J. Bunker, "Third Generation Gangs Strategic Note No. 22: Rio's Gangs Impose Curfews in Response to Coronavirus." *Small Wars Journal.* 10 April 2020, https://

smallwarsjournal.com/jrnl/art/third-generation-gangs-strategic-note-no-22-rios-gangs-impose-curfews-response-coronavirus; John P. Sullivan, Robert J. Bunker, and Juan Ricardo Gómez Hecht, "Third Generation Gangs Strategic Note No. 23: El Salvadoran Gangs (Maras) Enforce Domestic Quarantine / Stay at Home Orders (Cuarentena domiciliar)." *Small Wars Journal*. 5 May 2020, https://smallwarsjournal.com/jrnl/art/third-generation-gangs-strategic-note-no-23-el-salvadoran-gangs-maras-enforce-domestic; and Robert J. Bunker and John P. Sullivan, "Mexican Cartel Strategic Note No. 29: An Overview of Cartel Activities Related to COVID-19 Humanitarian Response." *Small Wars Journal*. 8 May 2020, https://smallwarsjournal.com/jrnl/art/mexican-cartel-strategic-note-no-29-overview-cartel-activities-related-covid-19; John P. Sullivan and Robert J. Bunker, "Third Generation Gangs Strategic Note No. 24: COVID-19, Gangs and Lockdown in Cape Town." *Small Wars Journal*. 18 May 2020, https://smallwarsjournal.com/jrnl/art/third-generation-gangs-strategic-note-no-24-covid-19-gangs-and-lockdown-cape-town; and Alexandra Phelan, John P. Sullivan, and Robert J. Bunker, "Third Generation Gangs Strategic Note No. 25: COVID-19, Revolutionaries and BACRIM in Colombia." *Small Wars Journal*. 2 June 2020, https://smallwarsjournal.com/jrnl/art/third-generation-gangs-strategic-note-no-26-covid-19-revolutionaries-and-bacrim-colombia.

[6] Anna Sergi, "Effetti indesiderati del Covid-19: sei opportunità per le mafie," [Undesirable effects of Covid-19: six opportunities for mafias]. *La Via Libera*. 19 March 2020, https://lavialibera.libera.it/it-schede-65-gli_effetti_indesiderati_del_coronavirus_le_sei_opportunita_illecite_per_le_mafie.

[7] Luca Rinaldi, "L'economia criminale del post-emergenza Covid-19," [Criminal economy post Covid-19 emergency]. *IrpiMedia*. 6 April 2020 https://irpimedia.irpi.eu/covid19-economia-criminale-post-virus/.

[8] Sara Amerio and Anna Sergi, "La Mafia Ai Tempi Del Covid-19: Espansione O Contrazione Degli 'Affari?" [The Mafia In The Times Of Covid-19: Business Expansion or Contraction?]. *Magistratura Indipendente*. 18 April 2020, https://www.magistraturaindipendente.it/la-mafia-ai-tempi-del-covid-19-espansione-o-contrazione-degli-affari.htm.

[9] Salvo Palazzolo, Palermo, "il fratello del boss della droga fa la spesa per lo Zen," [The drug boss's broche is shopping for Zen]. *La Repubblica*. 8 May 2020, https://rep.repubblica.it/pwa/locali/2020/04/08/news/palermo_il_fratello_del_boss_della_droga_fa_la_spesa_per_lo_zen-253439286/ and Salvo Palazzolo, "Palermo, spaccio di cocaina nel 'salotto' della città, 11 arresti. L'avvocatessa al pusher: 'Portami due pacchi di sigarette.,'"[Palermo, cocaine shop in the 'living room' of the city, 11 arrests. The pusher lawyer: 'Bring me two packs of cigarettes']. *La Repubblica*, 24 May 2020, https://palermo.repubblica.it/cronaca/2018/05/24/

news/spaccio_di_cocaina_nella_citta_bene_11_arresti_consegne_a_domicilio_per_ballerini_e_un_avvocatessa-197211783/.

[10] Anna Sergi, *From Mafia to Organised Crime: A Comparative Analysis of Policing Models*. London: Palgrave Macmillan, 2017.

[11] Lorenzo Tondo, "Mafia distributes food to Italy's struggling residents." *The Guardian*. 10 April 2020, https://www.theguardian.com/world/2020/apr/10/mafia-distributes-food-to-italys-struggling-residents#maincontent.

[12] Anna Sergi, *From Mafia to Organised Crime: A Comparative Analysis of Policing Models.*

[13] Lorenzo Tondo, "Mafia distributes food to Italy's struggling residents." The observation was made by Federico Varese. Nicola Gratteri, antimafia investigator and head of the prosecutor's office in Catanzaro, made the following observation in the same article, "Mafia bosses consider their cities as their own fiefdom," he added, "The bosses know very well that in order to govern, they need to take care of the people in their territory."

[14] Similar dynamics are at play as among organized crime groups globally. The COVID-19 Pandemic has exposed these tendencies as seen in the SWJ-El Centro case studies described at Note 1. For an example of the issues related to territorial control among gangs, see John P. Sullivan, "The Challenges of Territorial Gangs: Civil Strife, Criminal Insurgencies and Crime Wars." *Revista do Ministério Público Militar* (Brazil), Edição n. 31, November 2019, https://www.academia.edu/40917684/The_Challenges_of_Territorial_Gangs_Civil_Strife_Criminal_Insurgencies_and_Crime_Wars.

[15] Sara Amerio and Anna Sergi, "La Mafia Ai Tempi Del Covid-19: Espansione O Contrazione Degli 'Affari?"

[16] Salvo Palazzolo, "Palermo, i boss volevano lanciare una lista civica, 8 arresti. 'Se non c'è una candidatura giusta, siamo fuori da tutto,'" [Palermo, the bosses wanted to launch a civic list, 8 arrests. 'If there is no right candidate, 'we are out of everything']. *La Repubblica*. 27 May 2020, https://palermo.repubblica.it/cronaca/2020/05/27/news/palermo_i_boss_volevano_lanciare_una_lista_civica_8_arresti_se_non_c_e_una_candidatura_giusta_siamo_fuori_da_tutto_-257703229/.

[17] Carlo Macrì, "Appalti pilotati per favorire le cosche, arresti tra imprenditori e funzionari," [Contracts piloted to favor the gangs, arrests between entrepreneurs and officials]. *Corriere della Sera*. 28 May 2020,

https://www.corriere.it/cronache/20_maggio_28/appalti-pilotati-favorire-cosche-arresti-imprenditori-funzionari-c6cb4c8a-a0b4-11ea-9405-dd3eae1c39c1.shtml.

[18] Sergio Nazzaro, "Pandemia mafiosa," (Mafia Pandemic], *Polizia Moderna*, June 2020, https://poliziamoderna.poliziadistato.it/articolo/3535ed118c7b4065180711109.

For Additional Reading

Robert J. Bunker and John P. Sullivan, "Mexican Cartel Strategic Note No. 29: An Overview of Cartel Activities Related to COVID-19 Humanitarian Response." *Small Wars Journal*, 8 May 2020.

John P. Sullivan and Robert Bunker, "Third Generation Gangs Strategic Note No. 24: COVID-19, Gangs and Lockdown in Cape Town." *Small Wars Journal*, 18 May 2020.

Alexandra Phelan, John P. Sullivan, and Robert J. Bunker, "Third Generation Gangs Strategic Note No. 25: COVID-19, Revolutionaries and BACRIM in Colombia." *Small Wars Journal*, 2 June 2020.

Anna Sergi and Anita Lavorgna, *'Ndrangheta. The Glocal Character of Italy's Most Powerful Mafia*. London: Palgrave Macmillan, 2016.

Anna Sergi, *From Mafia to Organised Crime: A Comparative Analysis of Policing Models*. London: Palgrave Macmillan, 2017.

Part 2

Essays

Chapter 7

The Covid-19 Crisis and Future US National Security

Joseph J. Collins

First Published in Small Wars Journal on 13 April 2020

I have been sick since mid-March.

No, I don't have the Covid-19 virus, thank God, but I have had a month-long bout of nausea, anxiety, and mental discomfort. It is not the first time I had this condition. It began the first time on September 11, 2001 on the lawn adjacent to the Pentagon helipad. In the past month and the weeks after 9/11, both illnesses were caused by the frustration of knowing that, after spending hundreds of billions of dollars in the name of national security, the United States of America was again caught looking in the wrong direction at horrendous cost in blood and treasure. The US national security establishment has failed again.

In the last 20 years, we have twice suffered strategic surprise attacks. In each case, we were unprepared for what was an entirely foreseeable attack on the homeland. In each case, the national security bureaucracy—Defense, State, Intelligence, and various homeland security entities—paid inadequate attention to preparing for an event that its own Cassandras had declared as probable. In each case, hundreds of billions were spent on traditional, old fashioned missions and equipment, while inadequate sums were spent on preparing to fight the smaller but more vicious wolves closest to the sled. In each case, Americans died by the thousands on their own soil. In each case, we then spent trillions of dollars to combat the ill effects of an attack that could have been prevented or otherwise defeated.

We can do much better in securing our nation, but only if we open the aperture of national security and see the future problem set in all of its dimensions. With a severely damaged economy, the well-funded Pentagon is likely to be the biggest loser in the changes that will inevitably follow as the pursuit of national security expands beyond traditional national defense missions.

The Current Crisis

April 13, 2020 was an unheralded milestone. The Covid-19 pandemic in six weeks killed over 22,000 Americans, more than twice the number of Americans killed on 9/11 and in the wars in Afghanistan and Iraq that took place over the span of two decades. We are easily in sight of the sad day where we will lose more Americans to Covid-19 than we did in the Korean War.

Adding to this tragedy is the sad fact that most of our Covid-19 dead passed without their loved ones by their side. In New York City and other urban areas, the sight of makeshift morgues in refrigerated trailers haunts the nation. Nightly, the appearance on television of battle-weary doctors and nurses, some with inadequate protective gear, brings our blood to a boil and breaks our collective heart.

The United States had adequate warnings of a potential pandemic. The Swine Flu, SARS in various forms, and the Ebola virus events were all prior warnings to keep our guard up, our scientific agencies well-funded, our testing apparatus in fine tune, our personal protective equipment and ventilator stockpiles full, and our interagency "battle staffs" in good order. The last three US presidential administrations did almost none of these things.

Solid warnings of the danger of a pandemic came in early January, but rather than nipping the pandemic in the bud, President Trump, with the exception of the partial China travel ban, failed to act decisively in January and February despite repeated early warnings. According to a *New York Times* analysis:

> Throughout January, as Mr. Trump repeatedly played down the seriousness of the virus and focused on other issues, an array of figures inside his government … identified the threat, sounded alarms and made clear the need for aggressive action. The President, though, was slow to absorb the scale of the risk and to act accordingly, focusing instead on controlling the message, protecting gains in the economy, and batting away warnings from senior officials. It was a problem, he said, that had come out of nowhere and could not have been foreseen.[1]

By mid-March, the President became fully engaged in battling the virus, but by then it was too late to get out ahead of its spread. The United States now has more acknowledged infections than any country in the world. The apparent global death experience[2]—the number of deaths divided by the total number of identified cases—is in excess of 6 percent. On April 15th, the American death experience, has edged up to 4.3 percent.

Nations that acted early with rapid testing, tracing, and social distancing—South Korea, Taiwan, Singapore, and Germany, for example—have achieved much better results than the United States has. Nations that reacted slower than the United States had worse results. For example, Italy's death experience is over 12 percent, and Spain appears to be in similar trouble. In all, by Johns Hopkins-managed numbers published daily on CNN, by April 15th, there have been 2 million cases globally, with the United States accounting for more than 610,000 of the identified cases. (As is so often the case in global events, we cannot get the truth out of Russia or China.)

Changes Ahead

The human and financial costs of this pandemic suggest that significant changes are ahead for the U.S. national security establishment and the national strategy. National security must become the guiding principle, not just national defense. Defending the homeland means nuclear deterrence and defeating terrorists, but it also means defeating or ameliorating pandemics, dealing with climate change, and blocking the smuggling of narcotics. The following are but a few of the most likely changes that appear to be on the horizon. They may not all take place next year, but they are in the category of the nearly inevitable.

There will be much less money for traditional national defense programs at a time when the defense workload is great, and the federal budget already has a trillion-dollar deficit each year. The Pentagon will face significant resource challenges. It will have to adapt quickly and make deep, near-term cuts.

With at least 22 million Americans unemployed, tens of thousands of small businesses on the brink of bankruptcy, and numerous major corporations in need of bailouts, the federal government—already beset by large budget deficits—has spent additional trillions to send checks to individuals and make concessionary loans to businesses. At the same time, tax receipts will shrink from the economic slowdown. As the economy begins to recover, all cabinet departments are going to help to pay these huge bills in FY 2021 and beyond.

To make things worse, the clamor for "more stimulus" (and greater budget deficits) will be hard for this and the next administration to ignore.

The President will likely ask the Department of Defense to cut deeply into its next $700 billion+ budget request. With high optempo and demanding threats—China, Russia, North Korea, Iran, wars in Afghanistan and against terrorists in numerous countries—the Pentagon in all likelihood will have to cut spending deeply and (even worse) rapidly. It will hurt and not just for one budget cycle. The whole FYDP is under a cloud.

The Armed Forces will get smaller, optempo will likely go down, procurement will be cut back, and readiness spending will likely go down. At the same time, each of the services will likely have to shed manpower, the best way to rapidly cut expenses. Moving more capabilities into the reserve components will be a terrific way to save money, streamline active forces, and preserve capabilities for better days.

The Services rightly have tremendous duplication of capabilities. Which of these capabilities could be eliminated in favor of accepting more risk? For example, are there tradeoffs to be made among the services with their 3,311 fighter aircraft and 889 attack helicopters.[3] Can squadrons be eliminated or shifted into the reserves? Should we economize by eliminating MARSOC and putting those manpower billets back into an already shrinking Marine Corps? What new systems can be reduced in favor of service life extension programs for older but proven systems? Can we move even faster to a greater reliance on cheaper Unmanned Aerial Vehicles (UAVs)?

Over the past few decades, America's foreign policy has often led with the military. It would be wise in this time of adjustment to put the State Department back in the lead. Diplomacy can help to dampen international competition, save money, and relieve stress on a Pentagon that will be under tremendous budget pressure. While long-term competition with China and Russia will continue to have priority in the Pentagon, diplomatic initiatives could lessen the heat from Iran and North Korea, both of which are suffering mightily from Covid-19. Increasingly, many irregular warfare missions can be handled under train, advise, and assist, as opposed to getting US troops involved. The concept of by, with, and through local indigenous forces is already mature and should be maintained. US troops strength in Afghanistan and the Middle East should come down.

This would be an opportune time to make better use of our allies on low risk missions and to put more of the burden of collective defense on them. At the same time, the anti-alliance side of "America First" should be retired forever. We should save harsh words for our adversaries, not our allies. In a similar vein, we could lean more heavily on international organizations, like the World Health Organization, the World Food Program, and UN peacekeepers to take up the slack. While we pay the lion's share of their budgets, in the end, with careful oversight they can internationalize efforts, promote useful sharing of information, and save US resources.

The United States must prepare for pandemics and integrate climate change into its strategic planning processes. Non-traditional defense missions, such as support to civil authorities in pandemics, deserve greater attention.

We have seen the folly of keeping pandemic stockpiles and readiness at a low level. As battle staffs maintain peacetime readiness, coordinating elements for pandemics need to be on full time duty. Stockpiles must be filled. No state or federal entity can benefit from images of ventilator shortages or nurses wearing garbage bags instead of appropriate personal protective equipment.

We need a national pandemic plan. As we wargame military and terrorist attacks on the homeland, we need also to game pandemic responses so states do not end up competing for resources on a crowded international market. The results of those games should be used to refine the national plan. As in most successful federal plans, centralized planning and decentralized execution is likely to be the right formula for the federal-state-local response.

Support to civil authority missions need continuous reassessment and reinforcement. To do this, we need to make sure that National Guard personnel called to extended, active state or federal duty have access to TRICARE resources and support as necessary from the Army Medical Department. No Guardsman should ever have to worry about personal or family healthcare while on extended federal or state service. That said, both NORTHCOM and various state National Guard units have performed well, as did their active duty supporters from the Navy's hospital ships and the Army Corps of Engineers.

The United States needs a blue-ribbon commission to assess performance and outcomes in the Covid-19 crisis.

Crises in the United States from Pearl Harbor to 9/11 have generated major, commission-led studies. The Covid-19 crisis will require an epidemiological, medical, and policy review. It will have international, federal, and state dimensions. There isn't room in this paper to map out such a complicated effort, but the Covid-19 crisis will rank with major wars in its effect on the United States. It will be years before we have it in our nation's rear view mirror, and decades before we can no longer feel its crushing effects.

In summary, we were slow to gain our footing in this crisis, and we have suffered more cases of Covid-19 virus than any other country in the world. The disease has had horrendous costs in blood and treasure, compounded by its ill effects on our nation due to social distancing an a stalled economy. Our future efforts at national security must be broader than traditional national defense programs. Resource shortages will severely complicate Defense's challenging agenda in the years ahead. As we did after al Qaeda's attack on 9/11, a key step in regaining our footing will be to conduct a national, commission-led investigation into this crisis, not to assess blame, but to promote future national security.

Endnotes

[1] Eric Lipton, David Sanger, Maggie Haberman, Michael Shear, Mark Mazetti, and Julian Barnes, "He Could Have Seen What Was Coming: Behind Trump's Failure on the Virus," *New York Times*, April 11, 2020, 1.

[2] The actual death rates for Covid-19 will have to account for the total infected, those that died at home without being identified, as well as those who survived. The apparent death experience rate shown here is simply the ratio of deaths to those formally identified as suffering from Covid-19.

[3] IISS, *The Military Balance 2020* (London: Routledge for IISS, Feb. 2020), 27.

Chapter 8

When pandemics come to slums

Vanda Felbab-Brown and Paul Wise

First Published at The Brookings Institution Website on 6 April 2020
Reprinted with Permission of the Authors and The Brookings Institution

Slums provide uniquely challenging conditions for containing the coronavirus and confronting the threat of COVID-19. There may be no ambulances. No hospitals. No tests. No or few police. Only some of the most densely populated places on earth. When COVID-19 reaches the world's slums, few policy options are available; and those that exist often entail hellish bargains with the criminal groups that so often rule such areas.

Poor areas that surround the developing world's great urban centers are crowded places where one-room shacks may house a multi-generational family. They are deprived of public services, with water for drinking and washing often only available at communal distribution points. Sometimes, criminal groups in collusion with corrupt water authorities sell water from tankers or street carts. Washing hands diligently is impossible. Shacks lack toilets and entire neighborhoods have no sewage systems. Since households don't have electricity or refrigerators, stocking up on food is not feasible. In the absence of a safety net, staying at home can mean starvation.

Quarantine restrictions are compounded by the lack of official law enforcement. Social norms and the suppression of street crime are frequently provided not by police but by criminal or militant groups, even though they themselves are perpetrators of criminality and violence. In some cases, such as in Rio de

Janeiro's favelas, local criminal gangs have already taken it upon themselves to declare a coronavirus-related curfew, trying to mount some public health measures despite President Jair Bolsanaro's downplaying of the pandemic.

Criminal groups may even distribute some public resources such as water, soap, or food to families of the sick, seeking the political capital with which they rule slums. In other cases, governments and politicians who sometimes clandestinely, and other times openly, outsource the management of slums to criminal groups will explicitly ask these groups to contain the spread of COVID-19 in the areas they control. In some neighborhoods an enhanced police or military presence is considered predatory and would be met by local resistance.

Yet quarantine enforcement by criminal groups can be a dangerous strategy. Criminal groups can exploit the opportunity to eliminate their criminal rivals or opposition by civil society groups. They can use quarantines to tighten their hold on territories and the delivery of vital services and essential commodities, jacking up prices to prohibitive levels. Pogroms against ethnic minorities or migrants, falsely labeled as disease carriers, are a high risk in places such as India, Pakistan, and South Africa, where minority groups are routinely subjected to violence. Governments may ask criminal groups to restrict movement of the community members, secretly paying or encouraging criminals to act violently against anyone attempting to leave the slum-turned-ghetto.

When the virus hits these urban areas, the toll is likely to be catastrophic. There are few medical personnel or hospital beds, and likely no ventilators. Quarantined slum communities are not likely to have access to health systems built for the urban mainstream. The wealthy do not need to rely on public health provision, building their own clinics in their residences and buying up ventilators, as some of Russia's millionaires as allegedly doing. Unlike the global response to Ebola, COVID-19 is ravaging the entire world, including countries that have traditionally staffed and funded the few international humanitarian medical groups capable of deploying to underserved areas of the world.

The first task is to hold both the governments and criminal groups accountable for the health and security of the urban communities under their jurisdiction or control. To the extent that medical isolation facilities can be established, such efforts should receive priority. Criminal groups must be informed that they do not have carte blanche to exterminate their opponents or marginalized groups or hike up prices of commodities and medicines in the name of COVID-19 precautions; they should face special oversight and prosecution if they use lockdown enforcements for such purposes.

In contrast, humanitarian groups seeking to deliver medical aid in urban areas controlled by criminal or militant groups must be made immune from for providing material support to illicit actors. Such criminalization of humanitarian cooperation with these groups exacerbated the mortality from the famine that struck Somalia in 2011 and has hampered access for humanitarian personnel to needy communities in areas outside formal state control. To the extent that local, often informal groups, such as youth or religious groups, can be mobilized for the dissemination of COVID-19 information or service provision—such as food delivery—governments and international actors should provide oversight and negotiated security.

It is also essential to anticipate the development of an efficacious medication or vaccine. Such efficacy demands urgent provision. Yet the poor are often the last to get access. This must not happen again. The world must pay attention to the plight of marginalized urban populations and craft COVID-19 responses that can successfully navigate the complex health and security realities that define both their vulnerabilities and resilience.

Chapter 9:

Outbreak: COVID-19, Crime, and Conflict

Paul R. Kan

First Published at the Strategic Studies Institute, USAWC, Website on 14 May 2020
Reprinted with permission of the Strategic Studies Institute and US
Army War College Press, US Army War College.

The COVID-19 pandemic is the byproduct of illicit global trafficking. Although COVID-19 was likely transmitted to humans via pangolins sold in the wet markets of Wuhan, China, these markets acted as mere way stations for the virus. The natural habitats of the pangolins are the forests, grasslands, and savannahs of Africa. But, through a network of impoverished local communities, poachers, transnational organized crime, gangs and corrupt officials, approximately 2.7 million of this endangered species are captured and smuggled to Asia every year. The pangolin has earned the sad distinction of being "the most trafficked animal on earth."

The illicit global network of wildlife trafficking was a major facilitator of the pandemic, but the effects of the virus' spread are, in turn, facilitating more criminal activities while creating the potential for greater internal instability in many states. The contagion-crime nexus has been overshadowed by the urgent need to combat the spread of the virus. Nonetheless, COVID-19 is acting as an amplifier for crime and conflict that will have repercussions in the international security environment in the near and long term.

Raiding the Animal Kingdom

The global trafficking of pangolins was a highly lucrative business before the COVID-19 pandemic. Wildlife trafficking in general is not only profitable but is not punished as severely as trafficking in other illicit commodities. The combination of high profit and low risk has made wildlife the fourth largest illegally trafficked commodity in the world after drugs, weapons, and humans. At an estimated value of $7 to $23 billion per year, global wildlife trafficking provides the context to understanding how illegal pangolin smuggling created the conditions for the outbreak of COVID-19 and how organized crime will continue to bring violence to societies and undermine state governance.

The United States has recognized the significant power of wildlife trafficking and its ability to harm the stability of a number of countries. Congress passed the Eliminate, Neutralize, and Disrupt (END) Wildlife Trafficking Act in 2016, directing federal agencies to work to strengthen law enforcement, demand reduction, and build international cooperation and commitment. In fiscal year 2018, the US government dedicated approximately $122 million to combat global wildlife trafficking. This funding supports a multilayered approach that includes international, regional, national, and local actions to tackle the illicit worldwide trafficking of animals. The Department of Defense also plays an important role in combating wildlife trafficking. The 2015 National Defense Authorization Act specifically mentions that the DOD may support law enforcement missions around the world to counter transnational organized criminal activities including "the illegal trade in natural resources and wildlife."

However, both supply and demand incentives in the pangolin trade have made it resistant to US and other efforts to halt it. Trafficking in pangolins did not emerge solely from a demand in Asia for the mammal's purported medicinal benefits. When China banned sales of ivory, Asian organized crime adapted and engaged their African criminal counterparts to shift to the acquisition and selling of pangolins.

Transnational organized crime's role in wildlife trafficking has worsened challenges to state governance by weakening law enforcement and aiding violent opposition groups. In some cases, insurgent and terrorists groups have helped supply organized criminal gangs with illegal wildlife products. The outbreak of COVID-19 will continue to exacerbate these criminally generated effects.

Business as Usual During the Unusual

Operating as a "shadow state" in many countries, organized crime groups have long played a role in dealing with the repercussions of disasters. In the aftermath of hurricanes, floods, earthquakes, tsunamis, as well as during famines, disease outbreaks, and sudden economic downturns, criminal syndicates have helped to alleviate societal suffering in ways that governments have not. As a result, organized crime groups have been able to take advantage of societal disruption to further their interests at the expense of state legitimacy.

Although organized crime syndicates often act predatorily against people and businesses, they have nonetheless used their illicit supply chains to deliver necessities in uncertain times. After the March 2011 earthquake and tsunami in Japan, the yakuza mobilized a fleet of trucks to be the first to deliver food, bottled water, and blankets to hard hit communities. With their accumulation of illicit profit, organized crime groups have also been a source of capital for communities that have taken hard economic hits. During the 2008 financial crisis, the Italian mafia groups offered needed liquidity in the form of business and personal loans. The current pandemic has proven no different; Mexican drug cartels have been distributing similar humanitarian and economic relief in the form of food and cleaning supplies.

Far from being altruistic acts, criminal support for affected and vulnerable communities is a way for organized crime to continue to exert, and even expand, its power and legitimacy. Criminally supplied relief comes at a cost to be paid when legitimate emergency aid arrives in the form of reconstruction and business loans. Organized crime has routinely received a share of government directed emergency funds aimed at helping residents and legal businesses recover from disasters through bribery, extortion, and corruption.

Beyond gaining money from the diversion of government funding, organized crime has also found novel ways to generate illicit profit in crises. In the initial stages of the current pandemic, many organized crime groups' illicit activities were dealt a blow—the sudden disruption of the global supply chain affected their ability to transport and sell many illegal commodities. Drug traffickers have struggled to get needed precursor chemicals to manufacture certain narcotics and their customers have stayed away due to stay-at-home and social distancing restrictions. Criminal syndicates have quickly shifted to new black market opportunities such as counterfeiting personal protective equipment and disinfectant. Russian organized crime has assisted in diverting scarce ventilators to wealthy oligarchs who have links to the government.

Governments have not always taken a confrontational stand against organized crime groups in disasters and crises. In fact, states have also benefited from the community control that many criminal groups exert, this has been especially noticeable during the COVID-19 outbreak. Gangs in El Salvador have helped enforce stay-at-home restrictions while gangs in the *favelas* of Brazil are mandating more stringent measures than the government. The exertion of community control buttresses organized crime groups as alternate forms of governance and legitimacy in many countries.

The Coming of COVID Conflicts?

In a May webinar on "Corruption, Global Trade and COVID-19," Nikos Passas warned of emerging of "criminogenic asymmetries"—inequalities and gaps between the legitimate and illegitimate provision of scarce public goods leading to group grievances that feed violent movements. The sudden economic downturn and increasing private and public debt due to the COVID-19 outbreak has combined with the strain on people, businesses, and governments to create fertile ground for criminogenic asymmetries. Emergency measures to prop up economies have, so far, included broad discretionary power to distribute benefits, but will come with little political appetite for the slow-moving processes needed for transparency, oversight, and accountability. Such conditions will give rise to new criminal schemes to gain access to funds and resources that have reduced official scrutiny. As a result, government corruption is also likely to emerge. Increasing crime and government corruption will nurture group grievances and lend credibility to calls from violent actors to alter fundamentally the political status quo.

Group grievances surrounding COVID have already created simmering conflicts—leaders in Bolivia and Sri Lanka have used the outbreak to delay elections, leading opposition figures to claim widespread extraconstitutional manipulation of democratic processes. In the predominantly Muslim state of Gujarat, India, hospitals have been accused of "apartheid" for separating patients based on religion. Hezbollah has been able to gain access to highly sought after medical supplies and is utilizing thousands of its medical professionals to fight the pandemic, bolstering its status as an alternative to the Lebanese state.

The pandemic will also constrain the ability of political leaders to rely on traditional levers of power as in the past. The capacity of the police and military to manage conflicts and deal with crime will likely be diminished. State agents will be preoccupied with medical responses to the spread of the virus and hamstrung in meeting the growing social and political challenges. International organizations and non-governmental organizations that have worked to resolve internal conflicts will also be affected by the pandemic; their operations on the ground and on the frontlines will contract. Many international organizations and non-governmental organizations have already removed their personnel from conflict zones, not due to increased levels of violence, but because of health concerns related to the spread of the coronavirus. The United Nations announced an end to the rotation, repatriation, and new deployments of peacekeepers due to the spread of COVID-19, endangering fragile ceasefires and fresh transitional political agreements. Recognizing the unprecedented threat of COVID-19 and its intersection with violent conflicts, the UN Secretary General appealed for a global ceasefire.

Conclusion

The end of the pandemic will not mean that the crime and corruption associated with it will also come to an end. Even the development of a vaccine or a successful therapeutic regimen to prevent or treat COVID-19 will be subjected to criminal schemes; organized crime can divert medicine before it reaches the right populations or make counterfeit medicine to earn illicit profit. Seeking or finding treatments for COVID-19 may, therefore, also become part of future criminogenic asymmetries. Conflict zones will also reduce the access to populations when administering vaccinations or medical treatments, prolonging the pandemic in certain communities.

Without new strategic approaches to tackle the contagion-crime nexus, internal conflicts will blossom and haunt the international security landscape. International coordination is not only needed to find adequate medical solutions to COVID-19, but is also needed to reign in the criminality that fuels group grievances. One easy strategic approach is to raise the priority of illegal wildlife trafficking as an international and national security threat. The international community had treated wildlife as a lower tier illicit commodity to tackle. However, the current pandemic justifies the targeting of wildlife trafficking networks more fully and with a new sense of urgency. Preventing the next pandemic will require breaking the contagion-crime nexus, which may result in mitigating and stopping conflicts.

The US Army can play an important role in reducing global wildlife trafficking. The Army has many institutional links to military forces in source countries where endangered species are harvested and where well-armed poachers and technologically proficient criminal groups often outmatch local forces. With a renewed commitment to the training of local forces to take on wildlife traffickers, the Army can engage once again in a comprehensive program that focuses on operations like "casualty care in austere environments, mission orders, mission planning, key leader engagements, detainee operations, site exploitation, civil military operations, the fundamentals of patrolling, and tracking and operating geospatial equipment." Working with non-governmental organizations and conservation organizations that track and combat wildlife trafficking would also add to the Army's ability to understand current and emerging patterns and practices in the exploitation of endangered and rare species. As an institution, the Army can also provide training programs to dissuade its own Soldiers from obtaining endangered and rare species products in regions where they are serving and, therefore, reduce one part of the demand.

Elevating the contagion-crime nexus as a strategic threat is not just an issue of global public health or human security, but also a significant way to lessen the scope and scale of internal conflicts. With the world focused on combating the pandemic, the opportunity exists for the United States and the Army to take the lead in developing strategic approaches to stop, not only the next pandemic, but also the outbreak of fresh rounds of violent conflicts.

The views expressed in this Special Commentary piece are those of the author and do not necessarily reflect the official policy or position of the Department of the Army, the Department of Defense, or the US Government. This article is cleared for public release; distribution is unlimited.

Chapter 10:

Venezuela: Could the Coronavirus Threat Be an Opportunity

Keith Mines and Steven Hege

First Published at the United States Institute of Peace Website on 8 April 2020 and in Small Wars Journal on 11 April 2020

This article is cross-posted here with permission (on agreement) from the United States Institute of Peace

*A truce in the decade-long power struggle is urgent to fight COVID—
and could open a path to the nation's revival.*

Helping Venezuela resolve its political crisis will be vital to containing the potentially catastrophic COVID-19 pandemic there. A truce in the country's power struggle is urgent, and last week's U.S. proposal for a transitional government offers useful ideas, even for a naturally skeptical governing regime. Advancing them would benefit from mediation, perhaps by the Vatican or the United Nations, and will require cooperation among the major powers—the United States, Russia and China—involved in the crisis. If Venezuelans and outsiders can join against the common human threat of coronavirus, that could lay foundations for an eventual political solution to the decade of turmoil that has brewed the hemisphere's worst humanitarian disaster.

Venezuela's state of collapse will prevent many of its 32 million people from observing basic precautions such as social distancing and frequent hand-washing, making the country a special risk for COVID transmission. Most Venezuelans survive hand-to-mouth through daily hustles such as selling produce or contraband in crowded street markets and a third are malnourished, leaving their immune systems already depleted. Forty percent of households suffer daily interruptions in water supply and electricity. Even in the capital, Caracas, hospitals report they lack running water, sinks and soap, much less functional intensive care units or ventilators.

Remittances totaling $4 billion a year are now drying up as daily incomes evaporate for the nearly 5 million Venezuelan migrants and refugees who have fled the pre-existing crisis. With the tailspin in the global price of oil—and domestic refineries not functioning—massive fuel shortages are likely to impede access to basic staples in the near future. Widespread social upheaval could become uncontainable and serve to dramatically empower brutal criminal and armed actors.

A holistic response to the pandemic will require broad-reaching cooperation across Venezuela's political chasm. Unilateral humanitarian assistance by either side will fall woefully short. The U.S. proposal calls for both leaders with claims to the presidency, Nicolás Maduro and Juan Guaidó, to yield to a power-sharing government elected by the National Assembly—this following steps to return members from exile or detention and restore elements of the legislature's constitutional role that have been eroded during the long power struggle. The assembly would elect four members of a transitional council of state, two from the ruling party and two from the opposition. Those councilors would select as president a fifth member and would make decisions by majority vote. The body would oversee the crucial organization of parliamentary and presidential elections. The armed forces would be represented by a military advisor who would presumably be in a position to protect their interests throughout any transition.

These are essentially unprecedented parameters that have been put publicly on the table, although a similar proposal was floated privately by Guaidó's opposition interim government in negotiations last year. The proposal demonstrates clearly a U.S. endorsement for welcoming supporters of the Maduro regime—and its ideological base of Chavismo, built by former President Hugo Chavez—as meaningful participants in a revived democratic process. That notion of inclusiveness had remained ambiguous amid the conflict's deep polarization and zero-sum political rhetoric. The U.S. plan also is the first to offer sanctions relief incrementally as progress is achieved; prior policy had structured sanctions as leverage for the opposition until a full transition was achieved. The proposal likewise unlocks economic and humanitarian relief early in the process, with the condition that it be made "equally accessible to all Venezuelans," without political or ideological considerations.

It is so far unclear whether the U.S. proposal can reinvigorate efforts to facilitate the urgently needed truce between Venezuelan political forces. Maduro immediately rejected the proposal, which his party's intransigent hard-liners initially seem to have interpreted as an invitation for their surrender. This perception probably was not helped by the U.S. proposal having been sandwiched between indictments of Maduro and his inner circle the week prior and the arrival of a counter-narcotics flotilla off the coast of Venezuela days after. The lack of trust and simple communications between the United States and the Maduro regime will need to be bridged for the proposal to serve its purposes as a key reference point in hashing out desperately needed agreements among Venezuelans themselves.

In light of those challenges, there is a crucial need for a legitimate facilitator that can manage a complex process of negotiations that includes all the essential domestic parties with the clear endorsement of their foreign allies. Many players, such as the Organization of American States, have been compromised during the last year, but others, such as the Vatican or European Union, could re-engage. Both Maduro and members of the opposition had previously agreed that the Catholic Church could provide its auspices and moral authority in helping to usher in a short-term humanitarian agreement. And given the centrality of Russian and Chinese support for Maduro, a more robust role for the United Nations would be a true game-changer, particularly if it came with a Security Council resolution with the explicit support of all five permanent council members.

A key force in any scenario of renewed dialogue, both in the short and long term, will be the battered but still deeply motivated Venezuelan civil society. The groups that have been running soup kitchens in response to the economic crisis are now quickly switching to work against COVID, providing face masks and supporting medical facilities. Courageous and dedicated Venezuelans are showing the side of the country that will one day facilitate reconstruction—a selfless patriotism that shows a compelling love of their fellow citizens regardless of political affiliations. The country's most prominent civil society organizations—including many led by women, who have been long marginalized in politics—are also demanding that the regime and the opposition reach a humanitarian agreement to provide the country the immediate relief and future vision it desperately deserves.

Backers of both sides of Venezuela's political divide should listen to these inspiring voices and seek to reinforce domestic dialogue on an urgent truce to face the public health crisis as an initial step toward building a political way forward. If the U.S. proposal is inadequate, it should stimulate alternatives, based on its same inclusive spirit, to emerge quickly. The ticking time bomb of the pandemic simply does not allow the country to wait for the perfect conditions. COVID-19's conditions of force majeure can transform incentives to encourage immediate humanitarian cooperation and lay cornerstones for more comprehensive, long-term political solutions.

Chapter 11

The Coronavirus is a Call to Build Resilience in Fragile States

Nancy Lindborg

First Published at the United States Institute of Peace Website on 9 April 2020 and in Small Wars Journal on 10 April 2020

This article is cross-posted here with permission (on agreement) from the United States Institute of Peace

How the Global Fragility Act can pave a path forward.

As more developed nations have struggled desperately to contain and manage the COVID-19 pandemic, the specter of the virus rolling through the more fragile countries in the Sahel, Horn of Africa, and parts of the Middle East is a terrifying, slow-motion train wreck with the potential to trigger a devastating multidimensional-tiered health, economic, political, and security crisis. It also provides an urgent call to action to do things differently in fragile states so they can recover better.

Over the last two decades, fragile states have occupied significant attention as policymakers have sought to understand and address the core conditions that render these states the common denominator in a litany of global threats: terrorism, civil wars, extreme poverty, and yes, pandemics. More than 1.8 billion people live in states that are weakly governed or governed with policies that result in deep inequality and exacerbate social division. These states, frequently wracked by violent conflict, are especially vulnerable to the kind of shocks delivered by natural disasters or pandemics.

I witnessed this firsthand in 2014, when I ran the USAID task force for the Ebola outbreak in West Africa. As the crisis tore through three nations recovering from decades of vicious civil wars, the vulnerability of fragile states to these kinds of shocks was starkly illustrated. People deeply mistrusted their governments, ignoring the life-saving messages that could have more quickly stopped the disease from spreading. Accurate data was difficult to obtain. Families in crowded urban areas had little ability to separate the ill and dying. Police tried repressive tactics that backfired. And health systems were weak to non-existent for large swaths of the region.

These same conditions exist across a large swath of fragile countries, and this time, the virus, although less fatal, is what public health officials have feared most: potent and airborne.

As death tolls rise and economies crash across Europe and the U.S., the potential for COVID-19 to sweep through fragile environments without significant, effective assistance is a dangerous possibility. War has caused foreign medics to flee Libya, leaving behind a collapsed health system. In Venezuela, more than 30 percent of hospitals lack power and water, and 80 percent lack basic supplies or qualified medical staff. Sudan, currently in the middle of an historic, delicate political transition, has only 80 ventilators and 200 intensive care beds for its 44 million people. From refugee camps to slums across capital cities, citizens lack access to clean water and proper sanitation.

It is especially worrying that some governments are now responding with power grabs and severe measures under the cover of a health response. When commuters in Kenya were caught on the streets after curfew, Kenyan police officers fired tear gas into the crowds. South African police attacked homeless people with batons and rubber bullets only minutes after lockdown went into effect in Johannesburg. In Rwanda, there are reports that police shot and killed two young men found violating lockdown orders.

COVID-19 in fragile states presents an urgent crisis. But as Milton Friedman once said: "Only a crisis—actual or perceived—produces real change. When that crisis occurs, the actions that are taken depend on the ideas that are lying around. That, I believe, is our basic function: to develop alternatives to existing policies, to keep them alive and available until the politically impossible becomes politically inevitable."

In just the last year, a remarkable consensus has emerged among donor countries and multilateral institutions that we need to think differently about how to help fragile states. New strategies and frameworks by the United Kingdom, the World Bank and IMF outline similar approaches for aligning international strategies with a joint focus on changing the weak and often exclusionary governance at the heart of fragility. The World Bank's recent strategy on Fragility, Conflict and Violence recognizes that addressing fragility and reducing violence is key to ending poverty.

The U.S. Government similarly passed the landmark Global Fragility Act in late 2019, which calls for the U.S. Government to align security, diplomatic, and development action in a coordinated long-term strategy to address the causes of fragility and violence. The act calls for international coherence in strategies to create compacts with local actors to build more inclusive, more legitimate governance structures. In addition to an urgent humanitarian response, these are the strategies needed to combat the pandemic—not just to beat the virus, but also to ensure that fragile countries don't collapse under the crisis, further fragment into violence, or harden into repressive authoritarian governments that will perpetuate further cycles of violence and fragility.

Those countries most vulnerable to the impact of the pandemic will require significant support beyond humanitarian assistance, including debt relief and concessional financial support. Now is the opportunity to increase the effectiveness of this aid with coordinated international strategies that help strengthen institutions, increase equitable distribution of services and access to justice.

Two decades of evidence tell us that nations with high levels of social cohesion and citizen trust in their government are best able to withstand the inevitable shocks that batter us all. Now is the time for the U.S. to provide leadership consistent with the core tenants of the Global Fragility Act: coordinate international efforts in support of locally led solutions that strengthen state-society relations and create more resilient partners around the world.

Chapter 12

Cyber-States and US National Security: Learning from Covid-19

Jonathan Lancelot

First Published in Small Wars Journal on 20 March 2020

The Covid-19 disaster is a colossal international tragedy, a pandemic of epic proportions. This virus alone has challenged our way of doing business, politics, and war. Covid-19 started in Wuhan China in late 2019 and has spread exponentially around the globe. The World Health Organization (WHO) statistics state as of March 18, 2020, that there are 208,987 confirmed cases, 8,246 deaths from the disease, 1,787 asymptomatic cases, and only 606 self-reported positive cases. An international shortage of Covid-19 testing kits has made tracking and getting in front of the spread near impossible. There is no vaccine, and The US government has been trying to pass economic aid bills for Americans who are under a regiment of social distancing, rendering the economy to a near standstill. In short, humanity was caught off guard. This goes beyond our nation-state borders, culture, governments, and nationalities. So does the economic order of globalization, and cyberspace.

If this is not a warning for the Westphalian state system structure, it is a complete exposure of the vulnerabilities and weaknesses of nation-states in dealing with 21st Century challenges. In a world where transnational businesses cross borders, as well as international banking institutions, private military organizations, nongovernmental organizations, and individuals, nation-states who are self-interested, protective of their sovereignty, and seeking a dominant position within the international system have set themselves up for the decline. When nation-states decided to deregulate global markets and enter regional agreements like NAFTA and GATT, a situation solidified where international corporations determine the economic policies for weaker nation-states and benefit from the Washington Consensus. Without notice, the seed for the emergence of what I call cyber-states was planted.

Cyber-States can be borderless, composed of cyberinfrastructure and deep computer networks built into bureaucratic administrative structures and functions. Depending on the implementation of computer systems and advance mobile technology within a structure for governance, the power of administration could be in the hands of private contracting companies who innovate the technology or public officials whose jobs are made more accessible by utilizing the technology. Cyber-States would use systems like Estonia's e-governance and in a democracy, i-voting. Conversely, Cyber-States can utilize technology within an autocratic structure of governance, like China's social credit system, or artificial intelligence (AI) within its court system. Cryptocurrency systems coded by blockchain software create a digital currency, which could potentially be the central portion of a cyber-states power if there is public trust in the e-economy. Lastly, Cyber-States would utilize AI, automation, and machine learning in military weaponry like drones and robotics, and for a matter of circumstance, across the whole cyberinfrastructure for efficiency, and without latency. Conclusively, this would give technology companies a significant portion of distributed power within the functions of social governance, and traditional nation-state structures would be questionable at best.

What are the current implications for US national security? The first implication is our open market view of cyberspace and the sale of data by private social network companies like Facebook. Our national security is encumbered when private companies can use the data of citizens to sell to any entity who can pay, like the Cambridge Analytica case. If that data got into the wrong hands like North Korea, or terrorist organizations looking to coordinate a massive cyber or physical attack, how does that help US Cyber Command? The second implication is our bilateral relationship with China, which has a firewall surrounding its border, the opposite of our open worldwide network. The best solution going forward for the US would be for Congress to legislate a General Data Protection Regulation (GDPR) bill into law, providing the Department of Defense (DoD) more room to develop a proper cyber-defense strategy. The last implication is the current trend of the merging of AI into drone weapons, which could lead to fully autonomous weapons, which would be a disaster for diplomacy, international law including the laws of war, and the international system. Failed-States, more anarchy between societies, amplified globalization, increased instances of deadly pandemics, and an escalation of small wars will lead to the emergence of cyber-states within the next decade.

Chapter 13

Using Hybrid-Warfare Defeat Mechanisms to Fight the Coronavirus and Counter Future Bioweapons. A Novel Approach

Justin Baumann

First Published in Small Wars Journal on 12 March 2020

Introduction

This article attempts to produce a framework that can help public health officials and military leaders develop strategies and operations to counter and eradicate Covid-19 type viral pandemics or other future bioweapon threats we might face on the hybrid-warfare battlefield.

What is Hybrid-Warfare?

Hybrid-warfare is a concept that emerged just after the 2006 Lebanon War as a way to categorize and define unforeseen threats on that battlefield which characterized Hezbollah's defensive strategy against Israel. There is still a lot of debate about this topic, but we'll use the definition in Major Brian Fleming's 2011 SAMS monograph, The Hybrid Threat Concept: Contemporary War, Military Planning and the Advent of Unrestricted Operational Art:

> "As the military tried to define the threat in the post-Cold War landscape, numerous ideas emerged to better conceptualize the seemingly growing complexity of threat actors within the environment that did not conform to traditional enemy characterization. These

include the Three Block War, Fourth Generation Warfare, Contemporary Operating Environment, Network-Centric Warfare and most recently revisiting population centric Counter-Insurgency (COIN). The hybrid threat concept synthesizes relevant aspects of these constructs in conjunction with a pragmatic application of unrestricted operational art."[1]

Hybrid-warfare strategies allow us to tackle potentially unrelated and different threats in the same environment simultaneously while exercising unrestricted operational art. In hybrid-warfare, the problem sets for friendly forces can be found along a sliding scale of potential conflict environments and threats ranging from conventional to unconventional, as the diagram below illustrates. Each of these threats or conflicts can have their own PMESII characteristics.[2]

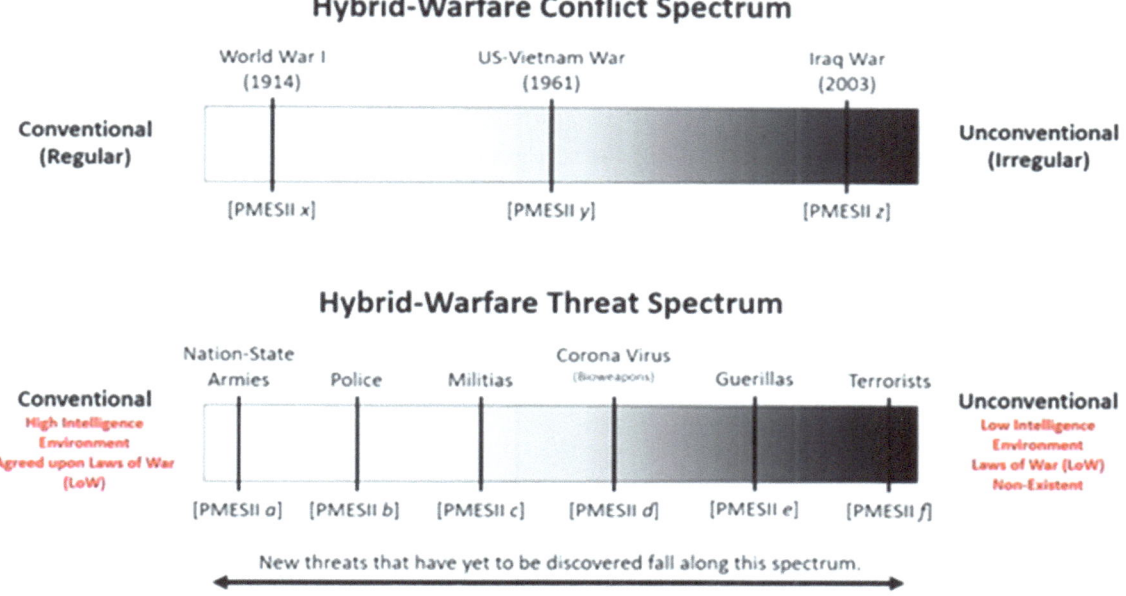

As we are seeing on the modern battlefield, it is incredibly difficult to predict where along the hybrid-warfare threat spectrum new hybrid-threats will appear, so it would be ideal to plan and prepare defeat mechanisms for all of the potential threats that could emerge along that spectrum. By applying this hybrid-warfare threat defeat mechanism methodology against the Coronavirus, we can tackle the virus using conventional and unconventional defeat mechanism strategies. These unconventional problems might be characterized as something like the burden on our healthcare infrastructure or transportation network disruptions; second and third-order effect issues related to viral infection. This concept helps provide a "benchmark" to begin to classify these conflicts and threats for greater defeat mechanism development.[3]

Defining Coronavirus as a Hybrid-Warfare Threat

By defining the Coronavirus as a hybrid-warfare threat, we can begin to identify the characteristics of how it wages war against us and then we can design defeat mechanisms to neutralize the threat. For instance, Covid-19 acts in very human ways because humans carry and spread the virus. The virus thus follows human movement patterns. This might sound obvious but can provide critical insight into applying non-lethal defeat mechanisms to isolate and quarantine the virus. This would have incredible legal, political, and social implications, but because of length, this article does not address those issues here.

Classifying the virus as a hybrid-warfare threat, we can also use this opportunity to ready our doctrine and forces in response to future bioweapon attacks by potential adversaries. There are rumors this may have been created as some form of a bioweapon, but the settlement of that issue is not relevant to our discussion here. Approaching this issue from a hybrid-warfare threat perspective however, we can more easily define and apply greater complexity to our national strategic response capabilities.

What are Defeat Mechanisms?

Major Douglas DeLancey's use of the CGSC Student Text Offensive and Defensive Tactics definition for "Defeat Mechanism" is a wonderful starting point:

> "The defeat mechanism is the singular action or pattern of activities by which a commander defeats his opponent. It is not a specific force or unit. The specific defeat mechanism adopted by the commander depends on the factors of METT-TC. The presence of different defeat mechanisms, along with changes in task organization, signals the onset of different phases of an operation. For example, the defeat mechanism for an attack is to maneuver to isolate a portion of the enemy force, leading to its destruction or rendering it ineffective. In an area defense, the defeat mechanism's primary pattern is to absorb the enemy's momentum as he moves into an interlocked series of positions from where he will be destroyed largely by fires. A defeat mechanism may combine several types or forms of operations."

Major DeLancey further describes Brigadier General (Ret.) Huba Wass de Czege's types of defeat mechanisms. These are Attrition, Dislocation, and Disintegration. While there are many different defeat mechanism models applied to warfare, we'll use de Czege's framework and these three defeat mechanisms to apply Hybrid-Warfare strategies against the Coronavirus.[4]

Applying these Defeat Mechanisms to the Coronavirus and Countering Future Bioweapons

> "These defeat mechanisms should be included in doctrinal publications that discuss planning operations. A widely understood, common terminology about how the commander desires to defeat his opponent will help planners select decisive points that achieve the commander's intent."[5]

Attrition: Quarantine Operations

> "Attrition as a defeat mechanism means fixing efforts at designated and advantageous locations and time to destroy [the enemy] forces faster than he can recover."[6]

In order to attrit the virus, self-quarantines over time by the populace can aid in long-term isolation of potential carriers. Self-quarantines are actions citizens can immediately take to minimize spread using social isolation. The sincerity of implementing one's own self quarantine will decide how much the spread is reduced. By taking proactive measures instead of reactive measures, overwhelming isolation will attrit the virus over time. This defeat mechanism provides long-term attrition of the virus as the probability it spreads from human to human decreases immediately. Digital remote workstations allow employees to work from home and still communicate quickly with other employees. These types of work-around measures will further reduce spread. Self-quarantine measures can be applied at all levels of managerial hierarchies across many industries and sectors.[7]

Dislocation: Offensive Operations

> "Dislocation seeks [to] rapidly [change] the conditions so that the enemy cannot seize the initiative."[8]

Governments at all levels can take steps to "dislocate" clusters of those infected by proactively instituting shutdowns of public congregating events like schools and recreational public gatherings and changing the conditions so the virus cannot spread. Closing borders, restricting transportation networks, and requiring additional testing all can aid in dislocating the virus from its aggressive interaction among humans. Testing is also an important component in dislocation. By revealing the existence of the virus in as many locations as possible, public health officials can design more efficient plans for medical assistance services and resource allocation. Digitized public network initiatives can help alleviate concerns about government preventing freedom of assembly.

Disintegration: Vaccine Operations

> "If well executed, forces can incapacitate enemy organizations and gain control of objectives. This defeat mechanism relies heavily on the destructive and shock effects of fire, followed closely by ground assaults."[9]

Creating vaccines can take time and should be included in long-term planning cycles. Vaccine operations as a part of a Disintegration defeat mechanism provide a more permanent solution to bioweapon threats and should absolutely be pursued. Supporting the Disintegration defeat mechanism could take the form of greater research dollars being spent or increased priorities for vaccine research. This defeat mechanism has a much longer payoff period than the other two but can be carried out concurrently. Anti-viral medication research testing would also fall under this defeat mechanism. By further developing those, Disintegration as a defeat mechanism is much easier to conduct against pandemic viral infections.

Conclusion

The work done by previous authors and researchers on hybrid-warfare and defeat mechanisms can provide a framework to build upon for tackling current and future bioweapon attacks as well as any unforeseen hybrid threats/actors on the battlefield. Applying these frameworks gives planners and strategists a starting point in approaching complex hybrid-threats from a proactive perspective. Attrition, Dislocation, and Disintegration are the canvas that the operational artist can use to devise solutions and strategies in creating winning scenarios against the threats that might appear in future engagements. Hopefully by working together and cross-sharing strategies and knowledge, we as a nation and global community can quickly eradicate this threat.

Endnotes

[1] Fleming, Major Brian P. The Hybrid Threat Concept: Contemporary War, Military Planning and the Advent of Unrestricted Operational Art., United States Army. 2011. pp. 3-4, http://cgsc.contentdm.oclc.org/utils/getdownloaditem/collection/p4013coll3/id/2752/filename/2753.pdf/mapsto/pdf.

[2] ADP 3-0 Unified Land Operations. United States Army. 2011. p. 2, https://www.army.mil/e2/downloads/rv7/info/references/ADP_3-0_ULO_Oct_2011_APD.pdf.

[3] Some people may not like using PMESII as a descriptive planning framework. Any planning organization or person can replace PMESII with their preferred method in describing hybrid-threat characteristics.

[4] DeLancey, Major Douglas J. Adopting the Brigadier General (Retired) Huba Wass de Czege Model of Defeat Mechanisms Based on Historical Evidence and Current Need. United States Army. 2001. p. 20, https://apps.dtic.mil/dtic/tr/fulltext/u2/a393858.pdf.

[5] Ibid., p. iii.

[6] Ibid., p. 22.

[7] Dr. John Campbell, https://www.youtube.com/user/Campbellteaching.

[8] DeLancey, Major Douglas J. Adopting the Brigadier General (Retired) Huba Wass de Czege Model of Defeat Mechanisms Based on Historical Evidence and Current Need. United States Army. 2001. p. 23, https://apps.dtic.mil/dtic/tr/fulltext/u2/a393858.pdf.

[9] Ibid., p. 25.

Part 3

Potentials

Conclusion

Gangs vs. States— The Battle Over the Contested Pandemic Space

Robert J. Bunker and John P. Sullivan

Los Angeles, California

10 July 2020

As this reader has shown, the COVID-19 pandemic has significantly impacted both sovereign state and violent non-state actors alike. Because of their entrepreneurial nature gangs—lacking in institutional inertia and hierarchical decision-making processes of states (both liberal democratic and authoritarian selectorates)—have been able to respond to the challenges and opportunities posed by the pandemic. Gangs, mafias, and other organized crime groups (OCGs) can act as criminal or gangster warlords and rapidly implement adaptive COVID-19 response policies.[1]

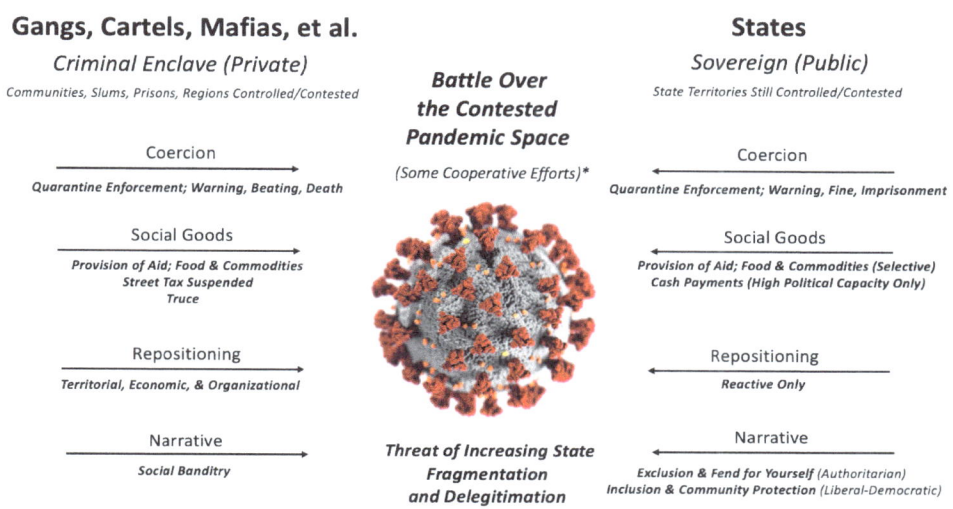

Figure 1. The Battle Over the Contested Pandemic Space

In the ongoing competition between gangs, other OCGs and states, the COVID-19 pandemic lays the foundation for amplifying the rise of proto state-making challenges, yielding the emergence of a new conflict zone. A "battle over this contested pandemic space" is now actively taking place. This contested pandemic space (described in Figure 1) pits gangs, cartels, mafias, and others entrenched in criminal enclaves (i.e., illicit privatized spaces including slums and prisons) against states and their sovereign (public) mandate. The contested or 'other-governed' spaces are the product of diminished state capacity and the rise of territorial (third generation gangs) including 'prison-street gang complexes' that dominate areas of weak and fragile governance.[2]

The major components of this new competitive struggle between gangs and states involve the utilization of coercion, social goods, repositioning, and narratives:

Coercion: The use of coercion within the pandemic space focuses on quarantine enforcement. Gangs and other criminal entities engage in such enforcement at a more blatant level of social control including symbolic violence. Groups identified as engaging in such coercive activities include *Comando Vermelho*

(CV) in Brazil, MS-13 in Central America, and *Cártel de Sinaloa* (CDS) and *Los Grandos,* a Beltrán-Leyva Organization (BLO) remnant, in Mexico. A shifting gray area exists where some of the criminal entities—certain criminal armed groups (CAGs) in Colombia and paramilitaries in Venezuela, for example—are acting under the pretense of supporting state authority or in actual coordination with some state officials (as in the case of political gangs in South America or where those officials have been co-opted by the criminal group) in their quarantine enforcement activities.[3]

Social Goods: For gangs and other OCGs, the provision of social goods typically includes the provision of humanitarian aid including food and necessities (e.g. so-called *'narco-despensas'*).[4] These can be sustained activities for the more strategically sophisticated organizations but are also commonly one-off or sporadic events that can be leveraged for their propaganda value via social and traditional news media. Such utilitarian provision of aid has been utilized by the *Cartel de Jalisco Nueva Generación* (CJNG), *Cártel del Golfo* (CDG), *Los Viagras, Cártel de Sinaloa* (CDS), *La Familia Michoacana* (LFM), a *Los Zetas* remnant in Mexico, various Cape Town gangs including the Americans and Hard Livings, and the Italian mafias (Sicilian mafia, Camorra, and 'Ndrangheta). At the same time, a 'street tax holiday period' has been declared in Guatemala during the pandemic by the *Sureños* and the *Revolucionarios* factions of *Barrio 18*. Gang truces—such as that enacted by Cape Town gangs including the *Clever Kids, Jesters,* and *Americans*—and a general truce with the state—enacted by the *Ejército de Liberación Nacional* (ELN) with the Colombian government (though not necessarily reciprocated by the state)—are also evident.[4] From the state side of equation, the provision of COVID-19 public aid is, for example, largely absent in Mexico—which many feel is playing into the hands of the cartels—although it is being used selectively for federal photo opportunities with SEDENA distributions apparent.[5] The same issues exist in Brazil and many other states affected by the pandemic where there is a lack of state economic resources and an unwillingness to support marginalized populations within authoritarian and populist regimes.[6]

Repositioning: Due to traditional illicit operations being curtailed and even suspended, many criminal groups are repositioning their activities. This repositioning is resulting in territorial, economic, and organizational changes. The better positioned Mexican cartels and Colombian CAGs, for instance, are moving against their criminal rivals as their states are preoccupied and overburdened with pandemic response issues, rising infection rates and death tolls, and further constrained budgets which is impacting law enforcement and military force activities focused on organized crime suppression. On the economic level, new ways to supplement lost revenues are actively and aggressively being explored. This includes creating new illicit trafficking routes, substituting (or finding alternative country sourcing) for some chemical precursors now in short supply for the manufacture of synthetic drugs, and capitalizing on the pandemic by selling knock-off masks and medicines. In the case of *Los Viagras*, a special COVID-19 street tax is being assessed while for others, such as the *La Unión Tepito*, there is an insistence that extortion payments must continue during the pandemic. Some criminal groups—such as the *Ejército de Liberación Nacional* (ELN) *Western Bloc* in Colombia—are taking a COVID-19 pause to retrain some of their field forces whereas others are employing new strategic business gambits.

While on one level the Italian mafia engaging in COVID-19 related loan sharking (bailing out failing businesses with high interest loans), further penetrating municipal administrations (in order to distribute public monies), and gaining a foothold in the health care sector appears to be simply new sources of revenue, these activities allow that mafia to reposition itself into entirely new segments of industry and governance, giving it new types of political influence. From a state perspective, however, such positioning is more difficult with the added burdens of territorial governance given the societal and economic disruptions taking place. No wide scale territorial offensives against gang and organized criminal enclaves or strategic repositioning of organizational structures appear to have taken place, rather states are trying to survive on a day-to-day basis and fall mostly into bureaucratic reactive modes in an attempt to weather the increasing COVID storm now raging within their sovereign territories.

Narratives: Gang and other OCG narratives frequently employ the 'social bandit' archetype identified by Hobsbawm.[7] The 'social banditry' construct is repeatedly referenced and exploited as criminal groups 'engage in the protection of their communities' by promoting the perception of keeping them safe from the effects of the pandemic through the provision of aid to the less fortunate, enforcing curfews and social distancing, forgoing street taxes, and even enacting gang vs. gang and gang vs. state truces (even if only honored by the criminal group) to alleviate general community pain and suffering during this time of crisis.[8] The juxtaposition of the gang narrative response to the pandemic 'in contrast to' the state use of such narratives is two-fold. In the case of authoritarian or transitional regimes with low political capacity, repression, and exclusionary policies, the benefits provided by public goods are limited to select political groupings and classes. This results in a mismanaged pandemic response or, perhaps more accurately, letting the mass of the citizenry fend for themselves. The policy of 'repression and exclusion' also fuels the 'fend for yourselves' response narrative in authoritarian contexts. In the case of liberal-democratic governance with high political capacity, freedoms and inclusion are meant to be the defining policy although, in the majority of the case studies highlighted in the notes section of the reader, the gangs and OCGs focused upon exist in states transitioning from authoritarian to liberal-democratic governance. These states have fragile institutions and a lack of governmental resources, due to underdevelopment, wide scale corruption by the political elites, and predatory plutocratic policies. Liberal-democracies, on the other hand, foster a narrative of 'inclusion' and 'community protection' that on one level can be considered 'institutionalized social banditry' derived from the perceptions offered by Tilly, Felbab-Brown, and others.[9]

Within this context, the observation by Nils Gilman that "the inadequacies of the response to the pandemic are accelerating the fragmentation and delegitimation of local, national, global governance institutions" results in 'alt-governance' actors filling the assistance vacuum left behind becomes increasingly important.[10] Authoritarian regimes of the low political capacity type that exist in Latin America are ill-suited to engage in the battle over the contested pandemic space with gangs and other criminal entities. The 'social banditry' narrative propagated by the gangs and other criminal elements at least offers disenfranchised social classes and communities some hope, however false, as opposed to the repressive, exclusionary, and 'fend for yourself' policies/narratives of the status quo political elites and populist politicians. It is only with the inclusion of liberal-democratic governance, both in those states within which it is firmly established and those transitioning authoritarian regimes where it is incipient, that the ability exists to provide valid alternatives derived from political enfranchisement, public goods inclusion, and community protection to stave off alt-governance proliferation and ensuing state fragmentation and delegitimation.

Endnotes

[1] For more on the selectorate theory in regard to authoritarian regimes, see Bruce Bueno de Mesquita et al., *The Logic of Political Survival*. Cambridge: MIT Press, 2003.

[2] See John P. Sullivan, "The Challenges of Territorial Gangs: Civil Strife, Criminal Insurgencies and Crime Wars." *Revista do Ministério Público Militar* (Brazil), Edição. 31, November 2019, https://www.academia.edu/40917684/The_Challenges_of_Territorial_Gangs_Civil_Strife_Criminal_Insurgencies_and_Crime_Wars.

[3] On the use of political gangs, see Max Manwaring, *Gangs, Pseudo-militaries, and Other Modern Mercenaries: New Dynamics in Uncomfortable Wars*. Norman: University of Oklahoma Press, 2020 (Reprint).

[4] David Lawler, "Mexicans offered little coronavirus aid as death and economic tolls climb." *Axios*. 29 June 2020, https://www.axios.com/mexico-coronavirus-response-amlo-lopez-obrador-d257b21a-fa29-4227-9f74-c476c8409ad0.html. SEDENA photo ops appear from time-to-time on

its Twitter stream (@SEDENAmx). See also Nick Schifrin, "In government's absence, Mexicans turn to cartels for pandemic aid." *PBS News Hour*. 7 July 2020, https://www.pbs.org/newshour/show/in-governments-absence-mexicans-turn-to-cartels-for-pandemic-aid.

[5] See Sandra Ley and Guillermo Vázquez del Mercado "COVID-19, despensas y narco." *CIDE*. 27 April 2002, https://www.cide.edu/coronavirus/2020/04/27/covid-19-despensas-y-narco/ and Ioan Grillo, "How Mexico's Drug Cartels Are Profiting From the Pandemic." *New York Times*. 7 July, 2020, https://www.nytimes.com/2020/07/07/opinion/international-world/mexico-drug-cartels-coronavirus.html.

[6] See, for instance, "Brazil's President Bolsonaro vetoes COVID-19 aid for Indigenous." *Al Jazeera*. 8 July 2020, https://www.aljazeera.com/news/2020/07/brazil-president-bolsonaro-vetoes-covid-19-aid-indigenous-200708190234748.html. The situation is so dire in some low political capacity states that large IMF aid packages are now being provided. "IMF approves $594 million in aid for Guatemala's COVID-19 response." Reuters. 10 June 2020, https://www.reuters.com/article/us-imf-guatemala/imf-approves-594-million-in-aid-for-guatemalas-covid-19-response-idUSKBN23H3L8.

[7] Eric Hobsbawm, *Bandits*. New York: Delacorte Press, 1969. See also John P. Sullivan, "Criminal Insurgency: Narcocultura, Social Banditry, and Information Operations." *Small Wars Journal*. 3 December 2012, https://smallwarsjournal.com/jrnl/art/criminal-insurgency-narcocultura-social-banditry-and-information-operations.

[8] Outlier behaviors still exist. La Familia Michoacana remnants have recently declared war on Fiscalía General de Justicia del Estado de México (FGJEM) component of the state in Mexico. See Veneranda Mendoza, "Familia Michoacana declara la 'guerra' a la FGJEM a través de narcomantas." *Proceso*. 7 July 2020, https://www.proceso.com.mx/637326/familia-michoacana-declara-la-guerra-a-la-fgjem-a-traves-de-narcomantas.

[9] Charles Tilly, "War Making and State Making as Organized Crime," in Peter Evans et al., Eds., *Bringing the State Back In*. Cambridge: Cambridge University Press, 1985: 169-186 and Vanda Felbab-Brown, *Conceptualizing Crime as Competition in State-Making and Designing an Effective Response*. Brookings. 21 May 2010, https://www.brookings.edu/on-the-record/conceptualizing-crime-as-competition-in-state-making-and-designing-an-effective-response/. See also, Vanda Felbab-Brown, "Foreword: Crime and State-making," in John P. Sullivan and Robert J. Bunker, Eds., *The Rise of the Narcostate (Mafia States): A Small Wars journal—El Centro Anthology*. Bloomington: Xlibris, 2018. pp. xxxvii-xliii.

[10] Nils Gilman, "Foreword: Pandemics and Conflict," in this work.

Afterword

Terrorism, Biosecurity, and COVID-19

Colin P. Clarke

Pittsburgh, Pennsylvania

3 July 2020

The novel coronavirus (COVID-19) pandemic continues to devastate the globe, ravaging nations large and small, rich and poor. One of the most poignant effects of the pandemic is that it has refocused counterterrorism analysts on the dangers of a potential bioterrorism attack, although the threat from malevolent actors seeking to use weapons of mass destruction (WMD) is hardly new.

In the past, groups like Aum Shinrikyo, al-Qaeda, and the Islamic State have all experimented, to varying degrees, with developing a range of WMD capabilities. Aum Shinrikyo explored the potential of weaponizing anthrax, botulinum toxin, and the Ebola virus, although the group's infamous 1995 attack on the Tokyo subway system involved the use of nerve gas.[1] Al-Qaeda and Osama bin Laden desperately sought nuclear materials, but were scammed on several occasions, in one case, ending up with red mercury, "a relatively notorious nuclear hoax."[2] Al-Qaeda also pursued a plot in the United Kingdom that was supposed to feature ricin, although the plot was disrupted in its early states. The Islamic State, for its part, is known to have looked into the concept of weaponizing the bubonic plague from animals that were infected.[3]

But among other examples, Aum Shinrikyo's failed biological weapons program highlights the difference between capabilities and intent. Indeed, compared to many other terrorist groups, Aum Shinrikyo boasted significant financial resources and impressive human resources, including access to scientists and other technically-skilled personnel. However, developing, acquiring, and deploying virulent strains of biological agents is challenging, even for the most capable terrorist groups.[4]

Even though there are serious challenges for terrorist groups seeking to improve their bioterrorism capabilities, the threat of bioterrorism, including the possibility of a clandestine, state-sponsored biological attack, has increased in part due to a combination of miniaturization, proliferation, and the manipulation of genetics.[5] Taken together, these factors diminish the probability of detection and enhance plausible deniability for potential attackers. Moreover, the ability of the United States, its allies, partners, and other sovereign states to limit access to potentially lethal biological agents is minimal, as these may be pervasive throughout the medical and research worlds.[6] Thus, bio-terrorism could be planned and carried out anonymously by a relatively small group, either independent or state-affiliated, with catastrophic results, given the difficulty of containing the effects, whether contagion of humans or animals, or contamination of food sources or medicines, etc.[7] Physical to digital conversion technologies, e.g., gene sequencing technology and the ability to send genomes by e-mail, is another growing area of concern where barriers to entry are being lowered, offering more opportunities for individuals and small groups to do harm.[8]

By witnessing how much damage and destruction the COVID-19 pandemic has wrought, this will likely accelerate terrorist groups' quest to develop or acquire a bio-weapon or to devote considerable resources into pursuing a bioweapons program. If a violent extremist or a member of a terrorist group were to successfully deploy a bioweapon in an attack, even if the attack itself fails to kill large numbers of people, the psychological damage—a major component of terrorism—will be significant and long-lasting.

COVID-19 has also exposed the deficiencies in many governments, which could further encourage terrorists to challenge the state. As populations lose faith in their governments, attenuated political legitimacy plays into the hands of violent non-state actors. This is particularly salient for those groups able to craft compelling narratives that offer current members and would-be recruits a cogent worldview in contrast to the state.

Along these lines, COVID-19 has been a boon for terrorist groups across the ideological spectrum, an extremists' buffet which allows each group to show their followers why their ideology is best equipped to explain why the pandemic occurred and how to successfully navigate a post COVID-19 world. As terrorism expert Magnus Ranstorp has pointed out, Salafi-jihadists have exploited the COVID-19 crisis for multiple purposes and see it occurring within a larger eschatological framework as divine punishment against infidels and destroying the West's societal infrastructure and economy."[9]

Anti-government extremists and those on the far-right may be the biggest winners, however, since widespread government ineptitude in responding to the coronavirus—from the United States to the United Kingdom, and from Brazil to Russia—has forced individuals to rely more on local communities, extended families, and informal networks. This contributes to a feeling of "every man or woman for himself or herself," and portrays the government as a parasitic or predatory element that taxes its citizens but is absent in times of need. Sub-state governance will receive a boost, and like-minded individuals and groups can connect both in person and virtually, strengthening transnational networks that exist outside of formal governance structures. White supremacists specifically, have demonstrated a desire to use COVID-19 as a form of a "bioweapon."[10]

With everyone stuck at home during quarantine and parents trying to both work from home and care for children, those kids considered self-sufficient—from ten years old to teenagers—are often left to their own devices, in the case literally. Millions are online and on their phones, spending hours each day in chat rooms and on gaming platforms.[11] COVID-19 will lead to economic turbulence and a continued growth in conspiracy theories, with rampant disinformation campaigns—some foreign-directed—further eroding trust between society and the government,

Many terrorist groups will be emboldened to move forward with plans to stage a bio-attack because they have seen the magnitude of which society can be disrupted as a pandemic spreads across the globe. After the attacks of September 11, 2001, at some point, life went back to normal, even as new security and screening procedures became commonplace at airports. But the change most are anticipating in a post-COVID 19 world is monumental. One of the refrains of policymakers in the immediate aftermath of a terrorist attack is to suggest that, no matter what, terrorists will not alter our way of life. But terrorist groups and terrorist attacks do alter the way we live. After 9/11, air travel was never the same. Even a cursory glance at dense urban areas in 2020 shows a drastically altered landscape in places like New York City's Times Square, which now includes concrete and steel jersey barriers and stanchions to prevent against vehicle rammings. Similar defensive measures have been adopted in European cities including Paris, London, and Stockholm in places where large crowds congregate. A catastrophic bioterrorism attack would have life-altering ramifications for how we organize our societies.

Part of terrorists' objectives in launching a bioterror attack is to provoke a massive overreaction. Marc-Michael Blum and Peter Neumann offer sage advice when considering how to conceptualize the threat of bioterrorism, noting, "rather than panic about terrorists engaging in biological warfare, governments should be vigilant, secure their own facilities, and focus on strengthening international diplomacy."[12] The aftermath of a bioterrorist attack would further strengthen terrorist groups in several ways. The lockdown imposed to respond and recover from an attack would provide terrorists with the opportunity to spread their propaganda, radicalize and recruit new members.[13] As authorities respond to the global health aspects of an attack, this offers groups the opportunity to launch follow up strikes as counterterrorism resources are diverted and depleted.

But just as terrorist groups will be emboldened to more aggressively pursue bioweapons following the COVID-19 pandemic, states, governments, private sector entities, and non-governmental organizations will also be reenergized to work toward preventing such attacks. More funding, a renewed emphasis on public-private partnerships, and a more finely tuned focus on training, equipment, and exercises—including between public health officials and counter-terrorism forces—should go a long way toward preparing the United States and the international community, writ large, for the inevitability of responding to bioterrorism wherever, and whenever, it eventually occurs.

Endnotes

[1] Angus M. Muir, "Terrorism and Weapons of Mass Destruction: The Case of Aum Shinrikyo." *Studies in Conflict and Terrorism,* 22:1, 1999, pp. 79-91.

[2] C.J. Chivers, "The Doomsday Scam," *New York Times Magazine.* 19 November 2015, https://www.nytimes.com/2015/11/22/magazine/the-doomsday-scam.html.

[3] Harald Doornbos and Jenan Moussa, "Found: The Islamic State's Laptop of Doom." *Foreign Policy.* 28 August 2014, https://foreignpolicy.com/2014/08/28/found-the-islamic-states-terror-laptop-of-doom/.

[4] William Rosenau, "Aum Shinrikyo's Biological Weapons Program: Why Did It Fail?" *Studies in Conflict and Terrorism,* 24:4, 2001, pp. 289-301.

[5] Paul Cruickshank and Don Rassler, "A View from the CT Foxhole: A Virtual Roundtable on COVID-19 and Counterterrorism with Audrey Kurth Cronin, Lieutenant General (Ret) Michael Nagata, Magnus

Ranstorp, Ali Soufan, and Juan Zarate." *CTC Sentinel,* Vol.13, Iss.6, June 2020, https://ctc.usma.edu/a-view-from-the-ct-foxhole-a-virtual-roundtable-on-covid-19-and-counterterrorism-with-audrey-kurth-cronin-lieutenant-general-ret-michael-nagata-magnus-ranstorp-ali-soufan-and-juan-zarate/.

[6] Richard Danzig, "Catastrophic Bioterrorism—What is To Be Done?" Center for Technology and National Security Policy, August 2003, http://www.response-analytics.org/images/Danzig_Bioterror_Paper.pdf.

[7] Jenna McLaughlin, "The Invisible Threat." *Foreign Policy*, 21 September 2017, https://foreignpolicy.com/2017/09/21/the-invisible-threat-biological-weapons-trump/.

[8] For more on the ability of individuals and small groups to wreak havoc, see Audrey Kurth Cronin, *Power to the People: How Open Technological Innovation is Arming Tomorrow's Terrorists,* Oxford: Oxford University Press, 2020.

[9] Paul Cruickshank and Don Rassler, Op cit, (Note 5).

[10] Alex Woodward, "Coronavirus: White Supremacists Planned to Use Virus as a Bioweapon." *The Independent, 22* March 2020, https://www.independent.co.uk/news/world/americas/coronavirus-terrorist-white-supremacy-fbi-bioterrorism-a9417296.html.

[11] "Game Not Over: An Assessment of White Supremacist Online Gaming," *The Soufan Center IntelBrief*, 28 April 2020, https://thesoufancenter.org/intelbrief-game-not-over-an-assessment-of-white-supremacist-online-gaming/.

[12] Marc-Michael Blum and Peter Neumann, "Corona and Bioterrorism: How Serious is the Threat?" *War on the Rocks*. 22 June 2020, https://warontherocks.com/2020/06/corona-and-bioterrorism-how-serious-is-the-threat/.

[13] Luke Baker, "Militants, Fringe Groups Exploiting COVID-19, Warns EU Anti-Terrorism Chief." Reuters. 30 April 2020, https://www.reuters.com/article/us-health-coronavirus-eu-security-idUSKBN22C2HG.

Postscript

Pandemics and Transnational Organized Crime

Tuesday Reitano

Geneva, Switzerland

6 July 2020

Criminal opportunism exploits systemic vulnerabilities

It feels too early to write a postscript on the issue of COVID-19 and organized crime. As the global caseload from the pandemic hits 10 million, confirmed deaths exceed half a million,[1] and many of the world's most populous and densely packed countries still to hit their peak transmissions, the narrative of the pandemic is far from over.

Analysts have described COVID-19 as a triple threat: a health, economic, and security crisis that is playing out simultaneously on a global stage.[2] The closure of borders and the locking down of public movement, and the challenges to governance that they have engendered, are reshaping the illicit economy as much as they are reshaping the licit, and just as the pandemic and its consequences are still evolving, so too are the evolutions to the illicit economy.

Organized crime is neither monolithic nor homogenous: it is made up of individuals and groups who have had different capacity to respond to the pandemic. But what the last half-year has made clear, however, is that criminal groups and illicit markets are far more innovative, robust and resilient than the states and institutions trying to control them. Lockdowns, curfews, social distancing and border closures have had a surprisingly limited impact on the operations of transnational networks, and in many ways they have created new opportunities and broadly served to benefit and strengthen local crime groups.

The missteps, preoccupation of state enforcement and the strain on the capacity of institutions has left too many opportunities and vacuums that organized crime was able to fill. And these were layered on top of existing and acute vulnerabilities in the infrastructure of the global economy and governance that have been created, often intentionally, in the last few decades.

There are, in my view, three major reasons why organized crime has profited and strengthened from the pandemic.

1. New criminal markets can be created overnight

The vast majority of criminal groups are poly-criminal, i.e., that they are able to earn profits and exploit more than one market. One key means by which organized crime groups (OCGs) proved their resilience during the pandemic was by shifting to or creating new criminal opportunities to sustain themselves when their primary markets were constrained by the pandemic. For example, a number of migrant smuggling groups whose industries were closed with the shutting of borders diverted to trafficking, trafficking groups have adapted to different forms of exploitation and online.[3]

The pandemic opened up business opportunities rapidly and at extraordinary scale, creating fake protective products, testing kits, medicines and miracle cures for the virus, as well as vending them online. Criminal groups manipulated markets to create demand, driving up profits, with traders based in China and Laos falsely marketing rhino horn products as cures for coronavirus.[4] In early March, a two-week law enforcement operation identified more than 2,000 links to products related to COVID, which is extraordinarily fast for a pandemic that was barely in the public consciousness in February. Cybercriminals stepped up the intensity of attacks on health sector and essential service institutions, reportedly recruited collaborators to help them maximize their impact, and offered ransomware as a service on the dark web.[5]

Governments fostered their own illicit markets: in South Africa a national ban on the sale of cigarettes and alcohol created an almost instantaneous black market with 200% or more markups and distribution of supplies being done by local gangs,[6] and as the US President advocated for hydroxychloroquine as a potential cure for the virus, pills were being offered on the dark web at 400 times their usual price.[7]

2. Global financial and regulatory systems do too little to constrain criminal opportunism.

Much of the ability of criminal groups to be so rapid and effective in their penetration of new markets comes as a result of the undermining of systems of regulation over the past two decades.

Whereas the movement of people was halted, the physical movement of necessary goods was eased, as governments sought to ensure necessary medical supplies could be procured, and that supermarket shelves would stay stocked in order to reassure consumers. Trusted trader programs that were designed to express goods through customs in order to meet just-in-time supply chains create surveillance weaknesses for trafficking groups to exploit.[8] Police report record sized seizures of cocaine into the EU during the pandemic, often disguised in foodstuffs and medical equipment.[9] The proliferation of global free trade and manufacturing zones have created massive blind spots for global enforcement, allowing illicit trade and trafficking to run rampant.[10] That the pandemic further weakened the capacity for trade surveillance, as port security staff were quarantined, furloughed or laid-off.[11]

Multiple weaknesses in database protection both in the private and the public sector and a lack of serious investment in cyber security for public institutions mean that people's identification is readily accessible for frauds of all varieties. Criminal groups have garnered hundreds of millions of dollars targeting federal assistance in multiple countries on every continent.[12]

Equally troubling is the clear evidence of federal money intended to purchase essential goods and equipment is too often being awarded to companies with insufficient qualifications, to the corrupt or the criminal. In Italy, the 'Ndrangheta was able to register itself as a pharmaceutical wholesaler and distributor to hospitals, purchase medical grade lifesaving drugs at the discounted rate, and has been reselling them onto the black market.[13] Corruption, failures in ensuring transparent public procurement systems, and the consistent failures to ensure clear beneficial ownership over corporations has resulted in systems that lack the integrity to meet needs in times of an emergency. This is reinforced by an international financial system that, by intentional design, is riddled with places to protect wealth in anonymity, and to avoid the payment of taxation. Designed for the wealthy and the privileged, tax havens, secrecy jurisdictions and lax requirements for corporate registration have also served criminal interests and enabled illicit financial flows.

What the pandemic makes clear for the first time—though it has been true for a long time—that this ecosystem directly results in the loss of life. It is laudable to see a limited number of governments taking a stand and denying bailouts to corporations registered in offshore tax havens, as it recognizes the harm that their practices of avoidance or evasion do to the development prospects of the countries in which they are physically based.[14] But a far more comprehensive reform will be needed to prevent this massive value diversion, and it would be positive if COVID-19 proved the catalyst of that sea-change.

3. Most states do not provide enough of a safety net in times of crisis

There is much that has now been written about how the pandemic is (like most shocks and contractions) is hitting the vulnerable hardest. The illicit flows that have disproportionately secreted wealth out of the global economy has left the majority of the population with no credible way to build a meaningful livelihood within the legitimate economy.

As a result of the pandemic, the World Bank estimates that the global economy will constrict by more than 5% this year—representing the deepest recession since World War II[15]—and the International Labor Organization (ILO) is predicting that up to 25 million jobs could be lost as a result of the economic disruption caused by COVID-19.[16] This is going to only expand the massive reservoir of vulnerability that organized crime will seek to exploit, in particular in the places where states and the free market provide too little in the form of relief.

Organized crime has stepped swiftly into the breach by providing welfare and proving their ability to deliver what states have not. The Italian mafia, the Japanese Yakuza, Cape Town gangs among others stepped in to deliver collections of food and PPE for local residents.[17] In Sinaloa, Mexico, the family of El Chapo Guzmán delivered care packages in boxes with the cartel kingpin's face etched onto them, so there would be no doubt as to where thanks were due.[18] This form of mafia welfare is a straightforward ploy to buy loyalty and build legitimacy with communities. It is the same well-proven strategy of criminal governance that the *maras* of El Salvador[19] and the Rio gangs[20] employed as they enforced lockdowns and policed curfews.

But where the behavior of gangs reinforces their hold in communities where they already have some authority, the pandemic may also offer organized crime opportunities to break new ground. Entire sectors of the global economy are under considerable strain and with insufficient availability of bailouts, sustained support, loans or lines of credit, business of all sizes are folding: all over the world, restaurants, shops, hotels, theatres, nightclubs, even sports teams have declared bankruptcy in the past few months.[21] For criminal groups this is an unprecedented opportunity to launder their money into the legitimate economy by offering high interest loans, or buying up failing business in cash.[22] Countries that have not had a long history of mafia presence may be unprepared to identify and respond to this kind of predatory behavior, lacking legislative framework and investigative experience,[23] while also still pre-occupied with dealing with the pandemic. By the time they come to grips with the scale of the penetration, it may well be too late, with entire communities tied into mafia ownership or indebtedness at a scale that will compromise legitimate governance.

A dire warning

This article is, indeed, not so much a postscript but a dire warning. There are many ways that organized crime is able to exploit and exacerbate human vulnerabilities and the structural conditions do little to ameliorate this reality. If this pandemic—and any other future shock to the global system—is not to result in a further strengthening of criminal groups at the expense of citizens of all walks of life, then we need to take urgent steps to reorient financial systems, provide proper safety nets and build sustainable, legitimate and dignified livelihoods, rather than continuing to hand the keys of the castle, on financial flows, trade, protection of privacy and identity to the wealthy and unscrupulous.

Endnotes

[1] "Coronavirus Map: Tracking the Global Outbreak." *New York Times*. 29 June 2020, https://www.nytimes.com/interactive/2020/world/coronavirus-maps.html.

[2] Alex Evans and David Steven, "Shooting the Rapids: COVID-19 and the Long Crisis of Globalization," *Long Crisis Network*. May 2020, https://www.longcrisis.org/download/.

[3] Livia Wagner and Thi Hoang, "Aggravating Circumstances: How coronavirus impacts human trafficking," *Global Initiative Against Transnational Organized Crime*. May 2020, https://globalinitiative.net/wp-content/uploads/2020/06/Aggravating-circumstances-How-coronavirus-impacts-human-trafficking-GITOC-1.pdf.

[4] "Coronavirus and rhino horn," *Save the Rhino*. 18 February 2020, https://www.savetherhino.org/asia/china/coronavirus-and-rhino-horn/.

[5] "Pandemic Profiteering: how criminals exploit the COVID crisis." Europol. April 2020, https://www.europol.europa.eu/publications-documents/pandemic-profiteering-how-criminals-exploit-covid-19-crisis.

[6] Nokuthula Khanyile, "Covid-19: Big profits for the cigarette 'black market' in KZN." News24, 9 May 2020, https://www.news24.com/news24/southafrica/news/covid-19-big-profits-for-the-cigarette-black-market-in-kzn-20200509.

[7] Marshall Cohen, "Trump mum on hydroxychloroquine as early trials falter but sick Americans still taking 'desperate measures' to fill prescriptions." *CNN Politics*, 24 April 2020, https://edition.cnn.com/2020/04/22/politics/trump-hydroxychloroquine-shortages-black-market-coronavirus/index.html.

[8] David Danelo, "For protection or profit? Free trade, human smuggling and international border management." *Global Initiative Against Transnational Organized Crime*. March 2018, https://globalinitiative.net/wp-content/uploads/2018/03/For-Protection-or-Profit-Intl-Border-Management-March-2018-web.pdf.

[9] Francesco Guarascio, "COVID 19: Latin American cocaine floods Europe during pandemic – some of it stashed in squid." Reuters, 30 April 2020, https://nationalpost.com/news/world/covid-19-latin-american-cocaine-floods-europe-during-pandemic-some-of-it-stashed-in-squid.

[10] *Governance Frameworks to Counter Illicit Trade*. Organizations for Economic Co-operation and Development (OECD). Paris: OECD Publishing, 2018, https://read.oecd-ilibrary.org/governance/governance-frameworks-to-counter-illicit-trade_9789264291652-en#page16.

[11] Bridget Johnson, "Maritime shipping and security weather a hard hit from coronavirus." *Homeland Security Today*. 5 June 2020, https://www.hstoday.us/subject-matter-areas/transportation/maritime-shipping-and-security-weather-a-hard-hit-from-coronavirus/.

[12] Mike Baker, "Feds suspect vast fraud network is targeting U.S. unemployment systems." *New York Times*. 16 May 2020, https://www.nytimes.com/2020/05/16/us/coronavirus-unemployment-fraud-secret-service-washington.html or Rafael Lima, "Online scams skyrocket during the COVID-19 pandemic." *The Brazilian Report*. 14 June 2020, https://brazilian.report/coronavirus-brazil-live-blog/2020/06/14/online-scams-skyrocket-during-the-covid-19-pandemic/.

[13] Sergio Nazzaro, Lyes Tagziria, and Ruggero Scaturro, "Parallel Contagion II" at "A parallel contagion: Is mafia entrepreneurship exploiting the pandemic?" *Global Initiative Against Transnational Organized Crime*. 11 June 2020, https://globalinitiative.net/parallel-contagion-mafia-covid/.

[14] Naomi Fowler, "A 'world fit for money laundering' must end in the post COVID-19 era." *Tax Justice Network*, 29 April 2020, https://www.taxjustice.net/2020/04/29/a-world-fit-for-money-laundering-must-end-in-the-post-covid-19-era/.

[15] "COVID-19 to plunge global economy into worst recession since World War II." *World Bank*. 8 June 2020, https://www.worldbank.org/en/news/press-release/2020/06/08/covid-19-to-plunge-global-economy-into-worst-recession-since-world-war-ii.

[16] "Almost 25 million jobs could be lost worldwide as a result of COVID-19, says ILO." *International Labor Organization*. 18 March 2020, https://www.ilo.org/global/about-the-ilo/newsroom/news/WCMS_738742/lang--en/index.htm.

[17] Sergio Nazzaro, Lyes Tagziria, and Ruggero Scaturro, "A parallel contagion: Is mafia entrepreneurship exploiting the pandemic?" *Global Initiative Against Transnational Organized Crime*. 11 June 2020, https://globalinitiative.net/parallel-contagion-mafia-covid/.

[18] Drazen Jorgic, "El Chapo's daughter, Mexican cartels hand out coronavirus aid." Reuters, 17 April 2020, https://www.msn.com/en-au/news/coronavirus/el-chapos-daughter-mexican-cartels-hand-out-coronavirus-aid/ar-BB12KzOz.

[19] John P. Sullivan, Robert J. Bunker and Juan Ricardo Gómez Hechgt, "Third Generation Gangs Strategic Note No. 23: El Salvadoran Gangs (Maras) Enforce Domestic Quarantine / Stay at Home Orders (Cuarentena domiciliar)." *Small Wars Journal*. 5 May 2020, https://smallwarsjournal.com/jrnl/art/third-generation-gangs-strategic-note-no-23-el-salvadoran-gangs-maras-enforce-domestic.

[20] John P. Sullivan, José de Arimatéia da Cruz and Robert J. Bunker, "Third Generation Gangs Strategic Note No. 22: Rio's Gangs Impose Curfews in Response to Coronavirus." *Small Wars Journal*. 10 April 2020, https://smallwarsjournal.com/jrnl/art/third-generation-gangs-strategic-note-no-22-rios-gangs-impose-curfews-response-coronavirus.

[21] Hank Tucker, "Coronavirus bankruptcy tracker: These major companies are failing amid the shutdown." *Forbes*. 3 May 2020, https://www.forbes.com/sites/hanktucker/2020/05/03/coronavirus-bankruptcy-tracker-these-major-companies-are-failing-amid-the-shutdown/ and Timothy Rooks, "Bankruptcy: Going out of business during the COVID-19 pandemic." *DW (Deutsche Welle)*. 17 June 2020, https://www.dw.com/en/bankruptcy-going-out-of-business-during-the-covid-19-pandemic/g-53823620.

[22] Sylvia Poggioli, "Coronavirus pandemic creates lucrative opportunities for organized crime in Italy." NPR. 17 June 2020, https://www.npr.org/2020/06/17/879041031/coronavirus-pandemic-creates-lucrative-opportunities-for-organized-crime-in-ital?t=1594020115404.

[23] Giuseppe Pipitone, "Spain, a safe haven for mafias in a mafia-free country. Under the shadow of the Kremlin." *il Fatto Quotidiano*, March 2017, https://www.ilfattoquotidiano.it/longform/mafia-and-organized-crime-in-europe/focus/spain/.

Appendix 1

U.S. Naval War College—Humanitarian Response Program—Pandemic Response: Select Research & Game Findings

First Published in Small Wars Journal on 1 April 2020

Introduction

This document is a summary of 16 key research and game findings focused specifically on the characteristics of civil-military response to a pandemic scenario. The numbered bullets below correspond to more detailed explanations of findings presented later in the document. While these findings are in no way definitive or complete, they are a sampling of relevant guidance based on research, gaming and expert opinion. It is our hope that these 16 findings will contribute to improving civilian and military effectiveness in humanitarian assistance and disaster response operations.

Note on Urban Outbreak 2019

The document references "Urban Outbreak 2019," which was an analytic war game designed, delivered and analyzed by NWC's Humanitarian Response Program in collaboration with Uniformed Services University of the Health Sciences (USUHS) - National Center for Disaster Medicine and Public Health (NCDMPH) and Johns Hopkins University's Applied Physics Lab. In September 2019, Urban Outbreak brought together 50 experts from five different sectors who averaged 10 years of humanitarian response experience. Over two days they gamed an infectious disease outbreak response in a notional but realistic city with a population of 21 million people. As part of the game, players individually voted for up to five essential organizations to which they needed access in order to complete the activities they deemed essential for success in the response. Histograms of those votes are offered in appendix I & II. The scenario-based aspects of the game that focused specifically on the unique characteristics of urban response in a widespread outbreak are also listed in appendix III.

Select Research & Game Findings[1]

Early actions and planning across all sectors are exponentially more important than reactive measures once the disease is widespread.

There will be intense and overwhelming demands for access to a few key health related organizations that are viewed as authorities in the early stages of a response. As the response moves forward, the number of stakeholders who are in high demand will increase and diversify.

While a response will often focus on serving the infected, any response must also focus on all the ways to lower the R "naught" or $R0$ (the average number of people infected by each new person infected). Regularly identifying high-risk practices that raise the $R0$ and replacing them with suitable alternatives for a population is an exceptionally difficult and absolutely essential factor for success.

Forced mass quarantine or other top down approaches to an outbreak that securitize the response with law enforcement and/or military enforcement may not be successful and could increase the spread of the disease.

Questioning the data central to planning and operations in an outbreak is an essential reflex that needs to be developed and sustained throughout an organization.

Currently, mortality is a better indicator of the scale of the COVID-19 outbreak than lab confirmed case counts. These facts on the ground are inherently lagging a couple weeks behind infections, but without real time and widespread testing of infections, mortality offers tangible and reliable data. Mortality "doubling time" is the most important and widely accessible metric for winning the race against COVID-19 in the absence of extensive testing.

Establish local media relationships early for risk communication as outbreak intensifies. In order to effectively combat misinformation and rumors, risk communication should be hyper-local, establish a track record for truth early, and directly involve known community members with a stated focus of honesty over polished language or production value.

Responders may be overconfident if they are not directly connected to the field. Frontline healthcare workers and first responders are often a good source of realistic assessments.

Personal and professional risk tolerance for humanitarian response activities is generally much higher for non-governmental organizations and medical first responders than it is for the military and U.S. government employees.

Even in the planning phase, the military and government may (consciously or unconsciously) exhibit avoidance behaviors to limit the scope of their involvement with affected and/or infected populations in the field.

A highly unusual mission and/or unprecedented response conditions such as pandemic response will meet with significant resistance, even among experienced professionals. This can directly inhibit effective planning and adaptation.

Private sector organizations are an absolutely essential and uniquely nimble component of any large-scale response. They must be integrated into planning throughout all phases of a response.

The U.S. government may need to clarify the difference between an "outbreak response" and a "humanitarian disaster" though these activities are not mutually exclusive.

Health care, drugs or other treatments should be provided through whatever means people are accustomed to within their local communities.

Social norms will change during a period of crisis; this demands careful observation and adaptation.

Responding organizations may not be aware that some response activities will not scale to meet the demands of an outbreak as they might for other disasters.

Expanded Findings

1. *Early actions and planning are exponentially more important than reactive measures once the disease is widespread.* Any containment strategy requires testing and tracing. This is not possible once a large enough population is infected. In the same way, altering business, social or cultural practices is significantly less effective when a society is facing a wide range of new challenges, especially severe economic and social pressures. Clarity, speed and repetition are essential for changes within a population and are most effectively achieved before other factors start making decisions for them. Generally, any action taken after a virus is widespread will be less effective due to the virus' impact on society. The larger and more complicated the action, the more the impact of the disease will be felt in its execution.

2. *There will be intense and overwhelming demand for access to a few key health related organizations that are viewed as authorities in the early stages of a response. As the response moves forward, the number of stakeholders who are in high demand will increase and diversify.* Urban Outbreak Example: After a shared briefing, 66% of the players voted that the Ministry of Health was the most essential stakeholder to which they needed access to complete their response activities during the initial outbreak. When players voted again after the briefing at the apex of the outbreak, their priorities for access had diversified by approximately 20% across a wider range of stakeholders. Players also voted to add approximately 30% more stakeholders as essential to their response activities. See histograms below.

3. *While a response will often focus on serving the infected, any response must also focus on all the ways we can lower the R0.* Pandemics are a function of human behavior mixed with a pathogen that has a specific R "naught" or R0. The R0 represents a simple average of how many people each infected person will infect. So R1.5 would mean everyone who gets the disease gives it to one and a half other people. The important thing to remember is the R3 means an exponential growth curve for the disease but it is not a fixed number. The R0 is a product of all the behaviors and environmental factors that result in those three new infections. So if society can change how they behave or alter the environment to lower that R3 to an R1 (or lower) while treating the infected, the disease will not be able to replicate enough to survive. In some cases this could be as simple as hand washing or social distancing, in other cases like Ebola it may clash with longstanding cultural practices like body preparation and burial by hand. Regularly identifying these high-risk practices that raise the

R0 and replacing them with suitable alternatives for a population is an exceptionally difficult and absolutely essential factor for success.

4. *Forced mass quarantine or any other top down approach to an outbreak securitizes the response. This may not be successful and could increase the spread of the disease.* Sick people actively seeking care, testing and public health messages concerning self-isolation and quarantine of contacts are the ways to end outbreaks. Forced mass quarantines are a direct barrier to those activities. One cannot slow the spread of disease if people hide infections out of fear or stigma. When authorities attempt to enforce a mass quarantine on a large population they will not be 100% effective. By stigmatizing the infection and symptoms they will teach others to hide their symptoms and drive key populations underground. This results in less sharing of information with authorities and medical providers, and the most desperate and the highest risk populations will seek to break quarantine.

5. *Questioning the data central to planning and operations in an outbreak is an essential reflex that needs to be developed and sustained throughout an organization.* Data collection, analysis and dissemination in a disaster response are by their very nature contentious political activities. Responders require data to execute their responses but rarely do the data collection and analysis themselves. This can lead to a significant weakness related to outbreaks as responders can base too many of their major decisions on external findings that may be dated, inaccurate, or misleading. Example from Urban Outbreak: There was no questioning or rejection of the epidemiological reports given to the players even though the infection curve did not follow the normal trajectory for this type of outbreak. This was especially apparent in the final round when there was no clear indicator of why the reported number of infections had fallen dramatically and yet many of the players embraced the idea that it was due to a successful response. This was concerning because designers anticipated questions about data collection and reliability by such a wide array of seasoned experts but not blind acceptance of such abnormal reports.

6. *Currently, mortality is a better indicator of the scale of the COVID-19 outbreak than lab confirmed case counts. These facts on the ground are inherently lagging a couple weeks behind infections, but without real time and widespread testing of infections, mortality offers tangible and reliable data.* While there is a great deal of data emerging about infection rates in the United States it is inherently behind the infection curve, incomplete and unreliable. For this reason, mortality is a better indicator of the scale of the COVID-19 outbreak than lab confirmed case counts. While even this number has

room for error and each death for COVID-19 is estimated to take 13-17 days - causing a long lag between interventions and results. It is more manageable data and allows rough calculations for decision-making. For example, instead of attempting to measure the number of infected, experts have offered that lengthening the number of days it takes mortality to double or "doubling time" is the most important and widely accessible metric for winning the race against COVID-19 in the absence of extensive testing. The further from three days the doubling time gets, the further a population is from the runaway period of the pandemic.

7. *Establish local media relationships early for risk communication as outbreak intensifies.* Urban Outbreak Example: Upon reaching the apex of the outbreak in round two NGOs and some U.S. Government (USG) independently identified a shift from national to local media outlets and dissemination, focusing on TV, radio, and billboards for "carpet bombing" public health messaging (as opposed to web, national or international) in order to build local trust, relevance, and community response rate. It will also increase a responder's control over speed of delivery and accuracy.

When focused on protecting public health, authenticity, truth and actionable information are the currency of successful risk communications. This is directly at odds with crisis communication, which is intended to shape messages to defend, protect or promote a particular brand or interest. In a sustained crisis the public will become increasingly dismissive of messages that don't reflect the immediacy or intensity of their experience or sentiments. In order to effectively combat misinformation and rumors, risk communication should be hyper-local, establish a track record for truth early, and directly involve known community members with a stated focus of honesty over polished language or production value. To maintain legitimacy in risk communication, inconsistencies in messages, response failures and/or public expressions of intense anger or grief should not be omitted or censored. Instead, they should be voiced, explained and offered as legitimate and understandable aspects of a community wide crisis.

8. *Responders may be overconfident if they are not directly connected to the field. Frontline healthcare workers are often a good source of more realistic assessments.* Example from Urban Outbreak: Players in round one (early onset) and round two (outbreak apex) were asked to rank their confidence in their ability to complete their priority activities if they had full access to those essential stakeholders they selected. In their post move survey they were asked to rate their assessment of the impact their

priority activities would have on the overall response. There was no significant change in confidence by any group except for Bravo Cell even though the outbreak grew exponentially. Participants in Bravo Cell – (NGO players), were statistically less confident in their ability to achieve their first priority activity between move one and move two. This confidence measure was from the only group focused on directly serving the affected population through medical care and other local programing. They were inherently more connected to the reality of directly running diverse patient-facing medical and public health programs. They are also highly aware of the personal risks they have to manage or mitigate as the programmatic leads in the field.

9. *Personal and professional risk tolerance for humanitarian response activities is generally much higher for non-governmental organizations and medical first responders than it is for the military and US government employees.* Urban Outbreak Example: Humanitarian organizations were significantly more engaged in the problem set on the ground than their military or government counterparts. While fully aware of security and logistical challenges in front of them, humanitarians and healthcare workers think in terms of baseline conditions for access, program rollout and sustainment first and consider complicating factors second. Military and government generally focus on authorities, mission parameters, personal security and other similar issues for an exceedingly longer time before even considering the functional factors involved in the effective execution of a mission or program. As the military and government engage in that early planning phase, they identify a great deal more reasons why they cannot do something rather than how they can. It is the opposite for humanitarians and healthcare workers because their work is predicated on the idea of responding unless there is an absolutely unacceptable risk. This can lead to cultural clash when collaborating. For example in Urban Outbreak, humanitarians became frustrated with discussion points offered by the military and USAID explaining:

"Health care workers don't need to waste time discussing coordination or mission drift – coordination is an activity you do and our mission is the population in front of us."

10. *Even in the planning phase, the military and government may (consciously or unconsciously) exhibit avoidance behaviors to limit the scope of their involvement with affected and/or infected populations in the field.* Urban Outbreak Example: This was highly apparent across a wide range of military and USG (e.g. CDC, HHS, USAID) players. Avoidance behaviors were most often exhibited as redirection of discussions and moves related to serving affected populations towards nebulous

high-level policy issues, minutia of command structures, and coordination imperatives. When pushed towards planning direct response activities, these players often used coordination with other "expert" organizations to passively externalize any personal or organizational risk of direct engagement with the population. The fact that these players knew the infection in the game was curable (with moderate immunity) with just two doses of antibiotics but actively avoided discussing distribution, or prophylactic force protection, lends credence to this interpretation. Humanitarians almost exclusively voted for affected/infected populations, as their most essential stakeholder to access, while other players did not vote for them at all. This shows a significant gap in the response community, as direct assistance to the infected will be a primary and overwhelming task in a pandemic.

11. *A highly unusual mission and/or unprecedented response conditions will meet with significant resistance, even among experienced professionals. This can directly inhibit effective planning and adaptation.* In the design and execution of the Urban Outbreak, experts at all levels sometimes vehemently rejected those game elements that they felt were too foreign to their experience. The original pathogen proposed for the game had an R0 closer to the COVID-19 virus, exhibited itself with cold and flu like symptoms, and required long-term intensive medical care for a small portion of the population. This proposal was rejected for a variant of a known and curable bacterial pathogen. The learning opportunity lost by failing to use the original pathogen proposed is now obvious.

    Urban Outbreak Example: During gameplay players would often exhibit physical discomfort and become argumentative concerning those aspects of the scenario that did not conform to their previous experience. This occurred even when other experts in the room would vouch for the scenario's veracity and relevance. The concern is that these reactions generally led resistant players to ignore or overlook good resources and guidance in their problem solving. If left unchecked it can often lead to a groupthink sentiment of "different is dangerous," with an obvious impact on effectiveness. This was exhibited in the game as key groups failed to engage in new and different aspects of the scenario (e.g. unique urban environment, mass antibiotic distribution, cooperation with local gangs) and instead retreated to exploration of known quantities, (e.g. C2 structures or information gathering activities).

12. *Private sector organizations are an absolutely essential and uniquely nimble component of any large-scale response.* Urban Outbreak Example: A lead for a private sector logistics company offered some of the

most tangible and innovative approaches to the problem set. The solution from his standpoint was to maintain business continuity (even while taking losses) by ensuring everyone on his payroll and their families had early access to antibiotics. He was confident his business would already have devoted members of local gangs and their families on the payroll as employees and so his early interest in their health and safety would open up the supply lines he would be able to use throughout the response. However, he had no interest in using overland shipping options due to security concerns and poor road infrastructure and instead sought to ferry all goods on waterways by employing a public private partnership with the local transit authority. With this strategy he was able to divide up most of the population centers and reach them without military support, air assets or many changes to his existing business model.

13. *The U.S. Government may need to clarify the difference between an "outbreak response" and a "humanitarian disaster" though these activities are not mutually exclusive.* Urban Outbreak Example: There was broad agreement among USG players that round one was an "outbreak response" which required more of a testing, contact tracing and health advisory role while round two was a "humanitarian disaster" requiring a different approach. There was still limited discussion of actually engaging the infected population. Priorities became personal security, disease surveillance, restricting movement by decentralizing resources, and looking for public health response mechanisms outside of health systems (e.g. sanitation efforts).

14. *Health care, drugs or other treatments should be provided through whatever means people are accustomed within their communities.* Urban Outbreak Example: In order to implement programs that are quickly accepted and effective with minimal disruption in dense urban areas, the international response needed to provide drugs, testing and aid through pre-established pharmacies, community organizations, religious leaders or practitioners without caveats.

15. *Social norms will change during a period of crisis.* Some changes may be characterized as normal coping mechanisms, but flagrant criminal activity must be actively pursued to reinforce social norms. The black market will inevitably become a critical factor as market pressures increase risk, reward and opportunity. Crime will also increase given the same factors, but including economic desperation and an opportunistic "testing" of authorities' control. Drug use, alcoholism and domestic abuse will noticeably increase. Every action by authorities may have magnified implications for individuals, families and communities.

16. *Responding organizations may not be aware that some response activities will not scale in the way that they normally would.* Urban Outbreak Example: Red Cross Movements continuously took the role of respectful and culturally appropriate mortuary affairs but they were never asked how they would manage disposal of 90,000 bodies in three months nor did they ever explain that capability. Under normal circumstances this wouldn't be an issue, but under extreme circumstances even highly effective and established organizations should reconsider their capacity over their capabilities.

Contributing Authors

Benjamin Davies
Kaitlin Rainwater Lovett
Brittany Card
David Polatty

Analytic Contributors

Alexandra Whiting
David Weinstein

A Note on Results Interpretation

The following histograms from Urban Outbreak 2019 show vote type and frequency from fifty players but they also show vote priority. Players were instructed that their vote order meant higher or lower levels of access to the external stakeholders they selected. A player's first vote was their highest priority stakeholder descending to their fifth vote. Players could choose from a list of 100 pre-identified organizations or add organizations. The first histogram shows the vote following the initial outbreak and activation of a response. The second histogram shows the vote at the height of the outbreak.

Appendix I

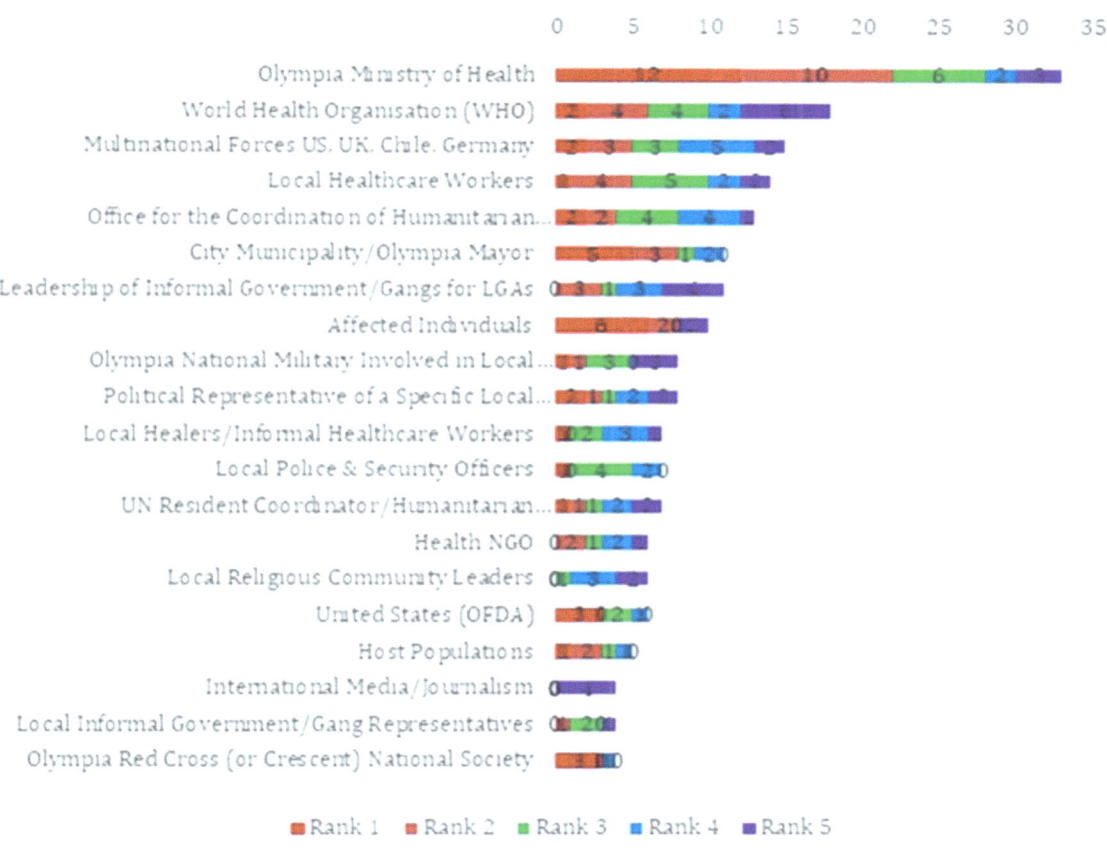

Appendix II

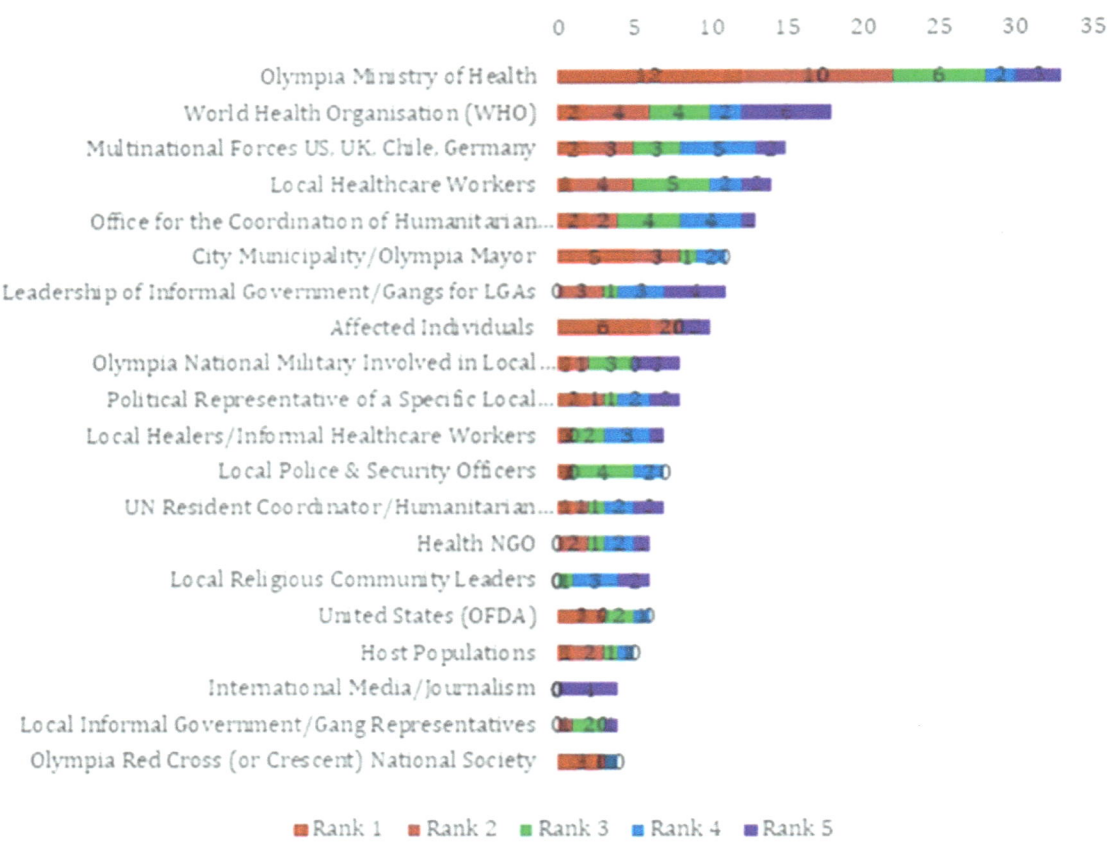

Appendix III

Urban Challenges and Areas of Inquiry in Urban Outbreak 2019 Scenario

Round One: Outbreak

- Concept of employing informal public health providers in the response
- Concept of informal governance/security for access or mobility for vulnerable populations in key dense urban areas
- Establishing role of private security
- Determining differential access to resources based on social strata and location
- Assessment data from rural mountainous region
- Self-interested government officials and private sector actors
- Prostitution as a vector
- False information/suspicion concerning the outbreak and response

Round Two: Cascading Failures

- Loss of power, utilities, dockworkers, security, etc.
- Failure of existing medical system
- All other medical services severely affected
- Logistical capacity stretched for outbreak response purposes at the expense of all else
- Hoarding, theft, and black market becomes extremely lucrative
- Increased international military role
- Challenges for responder security and ROE for military
- Ambiguous role of the national government
- Role of informal transit for response
- Flight of populations
- Quarantine/roadblocks
- Mortuary affairs
- PPE and medical demand

Round Three: Cleanup Wish List

- Pre-transition change in priorities
- Engineering, heavy lift or logistics from international military before transition begins/departure
- Reviving broken livelihoods
- Mortuary affairs
- Refuse in urban areas
- Security - rise of gangs and religious groups
- Badly damaged infrastructure
- Hobbled workforce
- Extreme needs associated with fractured health system (public health emergencies associated with those failures)

Endnote

[1] The views presented by the faculty and contributors do not reflect official positions of the Naval War College, DON or DOD.

SELECTED READINGS

Parker Asmann, Chris Dalby and Seth Robbins, "**Six Ways Coronavirus is Impacting Organized Crime in the Americas.**" *InSight Crime*. 4 May 2020, https://www.insightcrime.org/news/analysis/coronavirus-organized-crime-latin-america/.

Nicholas Barnes and Juan Albarracín, "**Criminal Governance in the Time of COVID-19.**" *Word on the Street (Urban Violence Research Network*. 6 July 2020, https://urbanviolence.org/criminal-governance-in-the-time-of-covid-19/.

Ryan Berg and Andrea Varsori, "**COVID-19 is increasing the power of Brazil's criminal groups**." *LSE Latin America and Caribbean Blog*. 28 May 2020, https://blogs.lse.ac.uk/latamcaribbean/2020/05/28/covid-19-is-increasing-the-power-of-brazils-criminal-groups/.

"**Beyond The Pandemic - How Covid-19 Will Shape The Serious And Organised Crime Landscape in the EU.**" Europol. 30 April 2020, https://www.europol.europa.eu/sites/default/files/documents/report_beyond_the_pandemic.pdf.

"**Bringing Within Reach: The importance of engaging armed non-State actors to tackle the COVID-19 pandemic.**" *Geneva Call*. 16 April 2020, https://www.genevacall.org/bringing-within-reach-the-importance-of-engaging-armed-non-state-actors-to-tackle-the-covid-19-pandemic/.

Counter-Terrorism Committee Executive Directorate (CTED), "**The Impact of the COVID-19 pandemic on terrorism, counterterrorism and countering violent extremism**." United Nations Security Council. June 2020, https://www.un.org/sc/ctc/wp-content/uploads/2020/06/CTED-Paper—-The-impact-of-the-COVID-19-pandemic-on-counter-terrorism-and-countering-violent-extremism.pdf.

"**COVID-19 Armed Non-State Actors' Response Monitor.**" *Geneva Call.* 15 May 2020, https://www.genevacall.org/news-covid-19-armed-non-state-actors-response-monitor/.

"**Crime and Contagion: The impact of a pandemic on organized crime.**" *Global Initiative Against Transnational Organized Crime.* 26 March 2020, https://globalinitiative.net/crime-contagion-impact-covid-crime/.

Benjamin Della Rocca, Samantha Fry, Masha Simonova, and Jacques Singer-Emery, "**State Emergency Authorities to Address COVID-19.**" *Lawfare.* 4 May 2020, https://www.lawfareblog.com/state-emergency-authorities-address-covid-19.

Steven Dudley, "**Latin America's Prison Gangs Draw Strength From the Pandemic.**" *Foreign Affairs.* 5 May 2020, https://www.foreignaffairs.com/articles/americas/2020-05-05/latin-americas-prison-gangs-draw-strength-pandemic.

Vanda Felbab-Brown, "**How COVID-19 is changing law enforcement practices by police and by criminal groups.**" *Brookings.* 7 April 2020, https://www.brookings.edu/blog/order-from-chaos/2020/04/07/how-covid-19-is-changing-law-enforcement-practices-by-police-and-by-criminal-groups/.

Vanda Felbab-Brown, "**U.S. Policing After Wave One of COVID-19.**" *Lawfare*, 20 May 2020, https://www.lawfareblog.com/us-policing-after-wave-one-covid-19.

Nathan P. Jones and Gary J. Hale, "**Organized Crime and the Coronavirus in Mexico.**" *Policy Brief 07.08.20.* Houston: Rice University, Baker Institute for Public Policy. 8 July 2020, https://www.bakerinstitute.org/media/files/files/f22f8c30/bi-brief-070820-usmx-organizedcrime.pdf.

Peter Katona, John P. Sullivan, and Michael D. Intrilligator, ***Global Biosecurity: Trends and Potentials***. New York: Routledge, 2010.

Kieran Mitton, "**South Africa's strict pandemic response could give criminal gangs an unexpected boost.**" *Washington Post (Monkey Cage).* 29 May 2020, https://www.washingtonpost.com/politics/2020/05/29/south-africas-strict-pandemic-response-could-give-criminal-gangs-an-unexpected-boost/.

Robert Muggah, "**The Pandemic Has Triggered Dramatic Shifts in the Global Criminal Underworld.**" *Foreign Policy.* 8 May 2020, https://foreignpolicy.com/2020/05/08/coronavirus-drug-cartels-violence-smuggling/.

Jonathan G. Odom, "**COVID-19 and the Law: A Compilation of Legal Resources**." 1 June 2020. George C. Marshall Center for Security Studies, https://www.marshallcenter.org/sites/default/files/files/2020-06/Odom_20200601_COVID-19_AND_THE_LAW.pdf.

Jania Pawelz, "**Why Coronavirus Gives Organized Crime Momentum to Shine and Flourish**." *Word on the Street (Urban Violence Research Network)*. 24 April 2020, https://urbanviolence.org/why-coronavirus-gives-organized-crime-momentum-to-shine-and-flourish/.

Luciano Pollichieni, "**Rule, Support And Buy: Making Sense of Mafia Strategies in the Covid-19 Aftermath**." *Word on the Street (Urban Violence Research Network)*. 19 May 2020, https://urbanviolence.org/rule-support-and-buy/.

John P. Sullivan, "**Criminal Insurgency: Narcocultura, Social Banditry, and Information Operations**." *Small Wars Journal.* 3 December 2012, https://smallwarsjournal.com/jrnl/art/criminal-insurgency-narcocultura-social-banditry-and-information-operations.

John P. Sullivan and Robert J. Bunker, Eds., **Strategic Notes on Third Generation Gangs**. Bloomington: Xlibris, 2020.

Back Cover Image: "Americans" gangsters, Cape Town. University of Cape Town Libraries, Independent Newspapers Archive. Source: African News Agency/ANA. Undated, https://digitalcollections.lib.uct.ac.za/collection/islandora-15160. [Used Under License].